Secrets of Insider Trader

Insight, Aspects, SCAMs, and Prosecution

Jatin Sharma

NewDelhi • London

BLUEROSE PUBLISHERS
India | U.K.

Copyright © Jatin Sharma 2024

All rights reserved by author. No part of this publication may be reproduced, stored in a retrieval system or transmitted in any form or by any means, electronic, mechanical, photocopying, recording or otherwise, without the prior permission of the author. Although every precaution has been taken to verify the accuracy of the information contained herein, the publisher assumes no responsibility for any errors or omissions. No liability is assumed for damages that may result from the use of information contained within.

BlueRose Publishers takes no responsibility for any damages, losses, or liabilities that may arise from the use or misuse of the information, products, or services provided in this publication.

For permissions requests or inquiries regarding this publication, please contact:

BLUEROSE PUBLISHERS
www.BlueRoseONE.com
info@bluerosepublishers.com
+91 8882 898 898
+4407342408967

ISBN: 978-93-6783-541-8

Cover design: Rishav
Typesetting: Sagar

First Edition: October 2024

प्रो. एस.पी. सिंह बघेल
राज्य मंत्री
मत्स्यपालन, पशुपालन एवं डेयरी
एवं
पंचायती राज मंत्रालय
भारत सरकार

Prof. S.P. SINGH BAGHEL
Minister of State for
Fisheries, Animal Husbandry & Dairying
and
Panchayati Raj
Government of India

Dear Mr. Jatin Sharma,

I extend my heartfelt appreciation for your exceptional work in authoring **"Secrets of Insider Trader - Insights, Aspects, SCAMs & Prosecution"**. Your expertise as a Supreme Court Advocate and your deep understanding of corporate and international law have resulted in a thorough and insightful examination of insider trading laws and prosecution strategies.

Your dedication to researching this critical topic and presenting it in such a comprehensive manner speaks volumes about your commitment to advancing legal knowledge and upholding market transparency. This book not only enriches the legal community but also serves as an important guide for corporate professionals and students.

Your hard work, research, and thoughtful analysis have made a significant contribution to the field of law, and I commend you for your tireless efforts.

Wishing you continued success in your future endeavors.

With best regards,

(Prof. S.P. Singh baghel)

Mr. Jatin Sharma
Advocate, Supreme Court of India &
Author of "Secrets of Insider Trader - Insights,
Aspects, SCAMs & Prosecution".

Office: Room No. 392, 'E' Wing, 3rd Floor, Krishi Bhawan, New Delhi-110001
Residence: 7, K. Kamraj Lane, New Delhi
Phone: 011-23782143, 23782548, 23782518, E-mail Id: mos-mopr@gov.in

Contents

Preface 1
About the Book 4
About the Author 6
A Dedication of Love, Legacy, and Eternal Inspiration 8
Introduction & Terminology... 9 to 29

Chapter 1
    Insider Trading: A Critical Analysis................................. 31

Chapter 2
    The Role and Importance of Stock Markets................................. 39

Chapter 3
    The Key Mechanisms of Stock Market Operations 51

Chapter 4
    Corporate Transparency and Financial Disclosure 63

Chapter 5
    The Anatomy of Insider Trading Policies 73

Chapter 6
    How SEBI Detects Insider Trading................................. 83

Chapter 7
    International Regulatory Frameworks for Insider Trading 93

Chapter 8
    Trading Mechanisms and How They Can Be Manipulated 103

Chapter 9
    Aspects of Insider Trading and Economic Impact 113

Chapter 10
    Prosecution and Legal Frameworks for Insider Trading............. 123

Chapter 11
    Landmark Insider Trading Judgments.. 133

Chapter 12
    Notorious Insider Trading SCAMs.. 143

Chapter 13
    Eye-Opening Insights: Why Insider Traders Sell Stocks 153

Chapter 14
    Insider Trading and Blockchain... 163

Chapter 15
    Criminal Aspects of Insider Trading 175

Chapter 16
    Practical Guidelines for Professionals and Investors................... 187

Chapter 17
    Corporate Governance and Insider Trading 197

Chapter 18
    Insider Trading in Emerging Markets... 199

Chapter 19
    Insider Trading and Corporate Social
    Responsibility (CSR).. 201

Chapter 20
    Technology and Insider Trading The Role of Fintech................. 203

Chapter 21
    Insider Trading Laws, Regulations, and Penalties
    Across Different Countries 205

Chapter 22
    Cross-Border Insider Trading: International
    Cooperation and Legal Challenges... 215

Chapter 23
Insider Trading in the Digital Era:
Cryptocurrency and NFTs 223

Chapter 24
Insider Trading and Technological Developments 227

Chapter 25
The Role of Whistleblowers in Insider Trading Prosecutions:
Legal Protections and Incentives 235

Chapter 26
Conclusion: Insider Trading – The Road to Ethical and
Compliant Markets 245

Chapter 27
Appendix: Supporting Materials for
Understanding Insider Trading 255

SAMPLE POLICY
Insider Trading Policy for Corporates 261

SAMPLE TRAINING MANNUAL
Employee Training Manual on Insider
Trading for [Company Name] 269

Key Resources for Further Reading 277

Preface

Insider trading stands as one of the most pervasive threats to the integrity and fairness of global financial markets. The term, often synonymous with high-stakes corporate malfeasance, involves the use of **material non-public information (MNPI)** by individuals to gain an unfair advantage in stock market transactions. Although insider trading scandals frequently make headlines and attract public scrutiny, the **real damage** extends far deeper, distorting the fundamental mechanisms that ensure market efficiency and trust.

This book, **"Secrets of Insider Trader: Insight, Aspects, SCAMs, and Prosecution,"** is not just another uncovering of insider trading scandals but it's a **comprehensive educational resource** designed to equip readers with the knowledge required to understand, identify, and navigate the complex world of insider trading. From **financial professionals** such as **Merchant Bankers, Chartered Accountants (CAs), Company Secretaries (CS), and Corporate Lawyers**, to **Stock Market Participants** and even the **general public**, this book aims to inform a wide audience about the **legal frameworks, regulatory practices**, and **enforcement mechanisms** that govern insider trading—both in **India** and on the **global stage**.

In today's fast-paced and increasingly digital financial environment, information is the "power". The **timing of information dissemination** can be the difference between massive profits and catastrophic losses. This is precisely why

insider trading is a critical issue—it enables individuals with privileged access to **sensitive corporate data** to leverage that information to **manipulate stock prices** and distort the market's ability to reflect the true value of securities. Such actions harm retail investors, institutional investors, and the market as a whole, undermining the principle of **equal access to information**, which is the bedrock of a fair-trading environment.

The importance of **regulatory vigilance** cannot be overstated. Regulatory bodies such as the **Securities and Exchange Board of India (SEBI) in India** and its global counterparts like the **Securities and Exchange Commission (SEC)** in the U.S. and the **Financial Conduct Authority (FCA)** in the U.K. have implemented increasingly sophisticated methods to detect, investigate, and prosecute insider trading. Despite these efforts, the allure of substantial financial gains continues to entice corporate insiders, traders, and others with access to **MNPI.**

The goal of this book is twofold. First, it seeks to provide **in-depth knowledge** of the **technical and legal aspects** of insider trading. The reader will explore **historical developments**, **case laws**, and **landmark judgments** that have shaped insider trading regulations. The focus will be on how SEBI and international regulatory bodies enforce rules to preserve **market integrity**. Second, this book aims to educate readers on **how to identify potential insider trading risks**, understand the penalties, and ensure they stay on the right side of the law. **Compliance** is not just a regulatory requirement but a "moral obligation" to uphold **market fairness**.

As markets become more complex and **financial crimes evolve**, the need for **education** and **vigilance** has never been greater. This book is your comprehensive guide to understanding the **secrets of insider trading**—not as a tool for exploitation, but as a defense against it. Knowledge is the most effective safeguard against financial misconduct, and with this knowledge, you'll be better prepared to navigate the ever-changing landscape of global financial markets.

About the Book

"**Secrets of Insider Trader: Insight, Aspects, SCAMs, and Prosecution**" is a meticulously crafted guide designed to provide readers with a comprehensive understanding of safeguarding from insider trading—one of the most contentious issues in the financial world. What sets this book apart is its **dual perspective** approach, making it equally valuable to **financial professionals** such as **Merchant Bankers, Corporate Lawyers, Finance Executives & Accountants, and Compliance Officers**, as well as **Stock Market Intermediaries & Investors** and the **General Public**. This book serves as a **practical resource**, offering both **technical insights** and **easy-to-understand explanations** that can be applied in real-world scenarios.

The contents are unique as at a time, it focusses on the **Indian Regulatory Landscape**, especially SEBI's proactive role in detecting and prosecuting insider trading and at the other end, it provides a **Global Comparison** by examining the **Securities and Exchange Commission (SEC)** in the U.S. and other major regulatory bodies like the **Financial Conduct Authority (FCA)** in the U.K. Readers will find in-depth knowledge on how insider trading cases unfold, from **Market Surveillance Techniques** to **landmark legal judgments** that have shaped the way insider trading is regulated & controlled globally.

What makes this book truly stand out is its use of **real-life case studies**—from the **Harshad Mehta scam** in India to the **Raj**

Rajaratnam case in the U.S.–providing a narrative that is not just educational but also engaging the readers. By incorporating the latest legal developments, technological advancements in market monitoring, and practical compliance guidelines, this book ensures that readers get **up-to-date legal perspective** on insider trading.

Whether you are a professional, looking to ensure compliance with insider trading regulations or an investor curious about the mechanism of market, this book will provide you with the **insights**, **deep legal analysis**, and **practical knowledge** that you won't find in other transcripts or knowledge materials. It's not just a book—it's a **comprehensive tool** for anyone who wants to understand and navigate the complex world of stock trading and its compliance pertaining to insider trading.

About the Author

Jatin Sharma, a distinguished advocate with over 12 years of expertise in Indian and international law, is the acclaimed author of *"Secrets of Insider Trader: Insight, Aspects, SCAMs, and Prosecution."* His academic journey is marked by excellence, holding an **LL.M. in Corporate Laws** and advanced specializations in **International Law** from Berlin, Germany, alongside qualifications in **Economics & International Business** from Dublin, Ireland. Further adding to his formidable credentials, he has specialized in **Conflict Resolution & Negotiations** from the prestigious School of Business and Administration, London.

His illustrious legal career encompasses a vast spectrum of complex legal domains, including **Corporate Law, International Regulations, Complex Commercial Litigation, Mergers & Acquisitions, Commercial Transaction Due Diligence**, and **Mediation & Arbitration**, among many others. This diverse expertise has established him as a leading authority in navigating intricate, cross-border legal challenges with precision and insight. His profound understanding of **corporate governance, global market regulation**, and **dispute resolution** has not only solidified his practice but also elevated his influence as a distinguished author, providing invaluable contributions to the legal landscape.

Jatin's prior work, *"Denial of Maintenance to Wife,"* became a best-seller, bringing him significant recognition for distilling intricate legal concepts into accessible and practical knowledge.

This success has solidified his reputation as a "Thought Leader" in both **contentious legal frameworks** and **corporate law**.

As the founder of **Jurist & Jurist International Law Firm**, his impact is recognized worldwide. His firm has been awarded by prestigious entities such as the **APAC Legal Awards (USA)** and **Lex Falcon (Singapore)** for its excellence in corporate law and international practice. His contributions to the legal field have been honoured by key dignitaries, including the **Lieutenant Governor of Mizoram** and the **Central Minister of Petroleum, Government of India**, reflecting his widespread influence.

Beyond his legal practice, Jatin is a passionate educator. His **corporate law courses** have empowered countless professionals to navigate the intricacies of modern business law with confidence and clarity. This dedication to education, combined with his professional excellence, has made him a respected figure in legal circles both in India and globally.

In *"Secrets of Insider Trader: Insight, Aspects, SCAMs, and Prosecution"*, Jatin Sharma combines his profound knowledge of **corporate law** and **global financial regulations** to offer a comprehensive analysis of compliances pertaining to insider trading, a critical issue in today's financial markets. His unparalleled experience in handling corporate cases related to insider trading makes this book an essential resource for professionals, legal practitioners, and anyone seeking a deeper understanding of the laws governing market fairness and integrity.

A Dedication of Love, Legacy, and Eternal Inspiration

This book, "*Secrets of Insider Trader: Insight, Aspects, SCAMs, and Prosecution*," is the culmination of countless hours of dedication, research, and passion. Yet, none of it would have been possible without the unwavering support of my family, friends, and associates, whose encouragement has been my constant source of strength throughout this journey.

I dedicate this work, above all, to the loving memory of **my father, Mr. Pramod M. Sharma,** who left for his heavenly abode 17 years ago. My father was not only a well-established and highly respected lawyer but also a beacon of wisdom, integrity, and compassion in our community. His legal acumen, coupled with his deep sense of fairness and justice, left an indelible mark on all who knew him. His unwavering commitment to the law and the values he embodied continue to guide me each day, both as a professional and as a person.

I also pay tribute to my grandfather, **Late (Dr.) M. C. Sharma, who served as the Chief Medical Officer (CMO)** before his retirement. His dedication to serving society through medicine was another profound example of integrity and compassion that I have been fortunate to inherit.

This book is a humble offering to my father's legacy and the principles he lived by. His love for the law and his relentless pursuit of justice are the foundations upon which this work is built. **To my father—my eternal source of inspiration—thank you**. This book reflects your legacy as much as it does my work, and I am forever blessed to carry your spirit with me in every step I take.

Introduction & Terminology

Introduction & Terminology

In order to understand the mechanisms of stock trading and insider trading with its legal implications, it's crucial to familiarize oneself with the core concepts of the stock market. This section introduces important terms that form the foundation of market activity, enabling readers to grasp how insider trading affects market behaviour.

1. The Concept of Stock Market and Its Importance

The stock market is the **financial backbone** of any economy, acting as a marketplace where companies raise capital by issuing shares, and investors buy and sell these shares based on market conditions. Stock markets are essential for:

- **Economic Growth**: By allowing companies to raise funds, the market fuels business expansion, innovation, and job creation.
- **Liquidity**: The market ensures that investors can quickly convert their shares into cash.
- **Price Discovery**: Stock prices reflect the collective sentiment of investors, influenced by public information, market forces, and economic trends.

In the context of insider trading, the stock market's efficiency is compromised when individuals, with access to **confidential, market-sensitive information**, manipulate stock prices for personal gain.

2. Definition of Key Elements of Stock Market

The stock market functions on a few key elements that keep it running smoothly:

- **Shares**: Ownership units in a company that investors buy or sell. Shareholders have a stake in the company's growth and profits.
- **Indices**: A group of selected stocks that reflect the market's overall performance, like the **Nifty 50** in India or the **S&P 500** in the U.S.
- **Securities**: Tradable financial assets, including stocks, bonds, and derivatives.

Regulators like **SEBI in India** and **SEC in U.S.** ensure that these elements function transparently, and insider trading is detected to maintain the integrity of the market.

3. Annual Report

The **annual report** is the official document that publicly listed companies issue each year to provide detailed insights into their financial performance, operational achievements, and future outlook. It includes:

- **Balance Sheets**: Outlining assets and liabilities.
- **Income Statements**: Providing details on revenue and profits.
- **Cash Flow Statements**: Showing how cash is generated and used.

For potential investors, the annual report is the primary source of information for making informed decisions. **Insiders** with early access to this data are legally prohibited from making stock transactions before the information is publicly released.

4. Arbitrage

Arbitrage is a strategy that capitalizes on price differences in different markets. It involves buying and selling the same asset simultaneously across two markets to make a profit. Arbitrageurs help keep markets efficient by balancing prices.

For example, if a stock is priced differently on two exchanges, an arbitrageur would buy at the lower price and sell at the higher price, making a risk-free profit. While arbitrage can seem straightforward, it becomes illegal if done with the advantage of **inside information**, especially during events like **mergers** or **earnings announcements**.

5. Averaging Down

Averaging down is a technique where an investor buys more of a stock after its price falls, lowering the average cost per share. For long-term investors, this can be a way to invest in companies they believe in, despite short-term price drops. However, if the stock price continues to decline, the investor risks significant losses.

If an insider employs this strategy knowing non-public information that would negatively affect the company, it would qualify as **insider trading**. Legal frameworks prevent insiders from making informed bets that the general public cannot.

6. Bear Market

A **bear market** refers to a prolonged period of declining stock prices, typically defined as a drop of 20% or more from recent highs. In such a market, investor sentiment is pessimistic, often driven by **economic downturns**, **high inflation**, or **rising**

interest rates. A bear market can last for months or even years, and it usually indicates broader economic issues.

In terms of insider trading, bear markets can exacerbate unethical behaviour, as company insiders may seek to sell off their shares based on non-public, negative information before the market reacts, which is a violation of **securities laws**.

7. Broker

A **broker** is an intermediary who executes buy and sell orders for clients, whether they are individuals or institutions. Brokers can be full-service (offering advice and personalized services) or discount brokers (offering basic trading services). They are essential to stock market functioning, as they ensure that transactions between buyers and sellers are completed smoothly.

Insider trading can involve brokers if they facilitate trades based on **material non-public information** provided by an insider. This makes brokers subject to stringent regulations under **SEBI** and **SEC** guidelines, requiring them to report suspicious activities.

8. Dividend

A **dividend** is a portion of a company's earnings distributed to shareholders, typically paid out quarterly. Dividends are often used as an indicator of a company's financial health. While many investors value stocks that pay regular dividends, companies can also cut dividends during financial stress.

Dividends are closely watched by the market, and insider trading becomes a concern when company executives, who know about upcoming changes in dividend policy (increases, reductions, or cancellations), trade shares ahead of public announcements.

9. Sensex

The **Sensex**, short for the **Sensitive Index**, is a **benchmark index** of the **Bombay Stock Exchange (BSE)** in India. It tracks the performance of 30 large, financially sound companies representing various sectors of the economy. Movements in the Sensex are seen as indicative of overall market health.

In terms of insider trading, any material information that could influence a Sensex-listed company's stock price is considered highly sensitive. Trading on such information before it becomes public would be a violation under **SEBI's insider trading regulations**.

10. Nifty

Similar to the Sensex, the **Nifty 50** is a **benchmark index** for the **National Stock Exchange (NSE)** in India. It consists of 50 of the largest Indian companies across multiple sectors. The Nifty 50 is a key measure of market sentiment and is widely followed by investors and analysts.

Insider trading concerns related to Nifty-listed companies are subject to **SEBI's strict oversight**, as these companies are often heavily traded, and price-sensitive information can lead to significant financial gains or losses.

11. Quote

A **quote** refers to the current price at which a stock is being bought or sold. It typically consists of two parts: the **bid price** (the highest price a buyer is willing to pay) and the **ask price** (the lowest price a seller is willing to accept). The difference between these two prices is called the **spread**.

In the context of insider trading, when insiders have material non-public information, they may manipulate stock prices by placing large orders that affect the bid-ask spread, creating false impressions of demand or supply.

12. Bull Market

A **bull market** is the opposite of a bear market, characterized by rising stock prices and strong investor confidence. Bull markets are often driven by **economic growth**, **low unemployment**, and **favourable business conditions**.

In a bull market, insider trading can take many forms. For instance, executives may sell shares before a major announcement that could temporarily halt the upward trend. Such practices are illegal and heavily monitored by regulators like SEBI and the SEC to ensure that the market's upward momentum is not artificially inflated by insider manipulation.

13. Bid Price

The **bid price** is the highest amount a buyer is willing to pay for a stock at a given time. It contrasts with the **ask price**, which is the lowest price a seller is willing to accept. The difference between the bid and ask prices can indicate market liquidity.

In the context of insider trading, manipulating the bid price through large buy orders before a major company announcement is a tactic used by insiders to influence market perception, making this a key area for regulators to watch.

14. Trading Volume

Trading volume refers to the total number of shares or contracts traded for a specific security during a given time period. High trading volumes usually signify strong investor interest, while low volumes suggest a lack of activity.

Unusual trading volumes, especially in the lead-up to earnings reports or other major corporate events, often raise red flags for regulators. Sudden spikes in volume without corresponding news can indicate that insider trading might be taking place, prompting further investigation by SEBI or the SEC.

15. Market Capitalization

Market capitalization (or market cap) is the total value of a company's outstanding shares of stock, calculated by multiplying the current stock price by the total number of shares. Market cap is used to categorize companies into **large-cap**, **mid-cap**, and **small-cap** groups, helping investors understand the size and risk profile of a company.

Insider trading can distort a company's market cap if insiders trade large volumes of shares before public news that will significantly affect the stock price. Such actions are heavily scrutinized by regulators to protect market integrity.

16. Intraday Trading

Intraday trading refers to buying and selling a security within the same trading day. Intraday traders aim to capitalize on small price movements by entering and exiting positions quickly. These trades rely on **liquidity** and **market volatility**.

In the realm of insider trading, intraday traders could exploit **non-public information** to benefit from short-term price changes, which is illegal under **SEBI's insider trading regulations**.

17. Market Order

A **market order** is an order to buy or sell a stock immediately at the best available current price. Market orders prioritize speed over price, making them suitable for investors who want to execute trades quickly.

For insiders, placing large market orders before public announcements based on **material non-public information (MNPI)** is strictly prohibited, as it can result in **market manipulation**.

18. Day Order

A **day order** is a type of order to buy or sell a security that expires at the end of the trading day if it hasn't been executed. It contrasts with **good-till-cancelled (GTC)** orders, which remain active until they are filled or manually cancelled.

For insiders, placing day orders ahead of anticipated news releases (using confidential knowledge) can lead to penalties, as it constitutes a violation of **insider trading laws**.

19. Limit Order

A **limit order** allows an investor to buy or sell a stock at a specified price or better. It gives the trader more control over the price at which the trade will be executed, but there's no guarantee that the order will be filled.

Insiders who place limit orders with knowledge of an impending price move due to non-public information could manipulate stock prices for personal gain, making such actions illegal.

20. Liquidity

Liquidity refers to the ease with which an asset can be quickly bought or sold in the market without affecting its price. Stocks with high liquidity can be traded in large quantities without significantly impacting the price, whereas illiquid stocks may experience larger price swings.

Insider trading becomes a concern when insiders take advantage of liquidity conditions, using their knowledge of non-public information to manipulate trades. SEBI and the SEC monitor liquidity trends to detect suspicious trading patterns.

21. Portfolio

A portfolio is a collection of financial assets such as stocks, bonds, mutual funds, and other investments held by an individual or institutional investor. A well-diversified portfolio can mitigate risk.

Insiders may manipulate their portfolios based on non-public information. For instance, if an executive knows that their company will announce disappointing earnings, they might sell stocks or rebalance their portfolio in advance—an illegal practice under insider trading laws.

22. Initial Public Offering (IPO)

An **Initial Public Offering (IPO)** is when a private company offers its shares to the public for the first time. IPOs provide companies with access to capital and give investors a chance to own a stake in the company.

Insider trading concerns arise during IPOs when insiders or underwriters involved in the process trade on non-public information about the company's potential stock performance. SEBI and the SEC have stringent rules to prevent such misconduct.

23. Secondary Market

The **secondary market** refers to the marketplace where investors buy and sell securities that have already been issued in the primary market (e.g., IPO). The most common secondary markets are stock exchanges like the **BSE, NSE, NYSE,** and **NASDAQ**.

Insider trading violations often occur in the secondary market, where individuals use non-public information to buy or sell shares. This type of trading is illegal and monitored by financial regulators globally.

24. Blockchain

Blockchain is a decentralized digital ledger technology that allows secure, transparent, and immutable recording of transactions. It has broad applications beyond cryptocurrencies, including **smart contracts** and **supply chain management**.

Blockchain technology is increasingly being explored to improve **market transparency** and **track trading activity**, helping regulators like SEBI and the SEC detect insider trading more effectively.

25. Blue-Chip Stocks

Blue-chip stocks refer to shares of large, established, and financially sound companies that have a long track record of reliability and profitability. These companies are typically leaders in their industries and offer **steady dividends** and **low risk**.

While blue-chip stocks are generally less volatile, insider trading in such companies is closely watched by regulators, as even small price movements in these stocks can significantly impact the market.

26. Capital Gains

Capital gains refer to the profit made from the sale of an asset like stocks, bonds, or real estate, where the selling price exceeds the purchase price. **Capital gains tax** is applied to these profits, and they are an important consideration for investors.

Insider trading laws prohibit individuals from using non-public information to generate capital gains, as it gives them an unfair advantage over the broader market.

27. Common Stock

Common stock represents ownership in a company and provides shareholders with voting rights at shareholder meetings. While common stockholders can benefit from **capital appreciation** and **dividends**, they are last in line for claims on assets in case of company liquidation.

Insiders with access to non-public information about a company's performance are prohibited from trading common stock based on that information, as it constitutes a violation of **securities laws**.

28. Current Ratio

The **current ratio** is a financial metric that measures a company's ability to pay off its short-term liabilities with its short-term assets. It is a key indicator of liquidity and is used by investors to assess a company's financial health.

Insider trading concerns can arise if executives trade stocks based on non-public financial data, such as a sudden change in the company's liquidity position before an official earnings release.

Key Terminology and Abbreviations

This section introduces key financial and regulatory terms essential for understanding **insider trading**, the **regulatory landscape**, and how modern **surveillance technologies** are used to detect and prevent market abuse. These terms are crucial not only for professionals working in corporate governance, securities law, and financial compliance, but also for general investors who want to understand the **complexities of market regulations**.

MNPI: Material Non-Public Information

Material Non-Public Information (MNPI) is at the core of insider trading regulations. It refers to any **confidential, non-public information** about a company that, if made public, would likely have a significant effect on its stock price. In other words, MNPI is information that can give an unfair advantage to individuals who trade on it before it becomes public knowledge.

Key Characteristics of MNPI:

- **Materiality**: The information must be significant enough to influence an investor's decision to buy, sell, or hold a security. For example, earnings reports, mergers, acquisitions, or regulatory approvals can all be considered material information.

- **Non-Public**: The information must not yet be available to the public through official channels like press releases, regulatory filings (e.g., **Form 10-K** or **Form 8-K** in the U.S.), or corporate announcements.

Examples of MNPI:

- **Earnings Announcements**: Knowing in advance whether a company will meet, exceed, or miss its earnings expectations can drastically affect stock prices.

- **Mergers and Acquisitions**: Information about an upcoming merger or acquisition can cause a company's stock to surge or plummet.

- **Regulatory Approvals**: For example, knowledge of FDA approval (for pharmaceutical companies) or environmental clearance (for industrial firms) can greatly impact stock values.

Legal Implications:

Using MNPI for trading violates insider trading laws, such as **Section 15G of the SEBI Act** in India and **Rule 10b-5** under the **U.S. Securities Exchange Act of 1934**. The penalties for insider trading based on MNPI can be severe, including substantial fines and imprisonment.

- In India, SEBI's **Prohibition of Insider Trading Regulations, 2015** explicitly defines MNPI and prohibits its misuse.

- In the U.S., the **SEC** prosecutes insider trading cases based on MNPI under **Rule 10b-5**, which makes it illegal to commit fraud or deceit in connection with securities transactions.

SEBI: Securities and Exchange Board of India

The **Securities and Exchange Board of India (SEBI)** is the principal regulatory authority responsible for overseeing and regulating the securities markets in India. Established in 1988 and given statutory powers through the **SEBI Act of 1992**, SEBI ensures the smooth operation of financial markets and protects the interests of investors. SEBI's role is critical in maintaining **market transparency** and **investor confidence** in India.

Key Responsibilities of SEBI:

- **Regulating stock exchanges**: SEBI ensures that exchanges like the **National Stock Exchange (NSE)** and the **Bombay Stock Exchange (BSE)** operate transparently and fairly.

- **Protecting investors**: SEBI's regulations are designed to prevent fraudulent activities like **insider trading**, **market manipulation**, and **corporate fraud**.

- **Enforcing insider trading laws**: Through the **Prohibition of Insider Trading Regulations (2015)**, SEBI defines who constitutes an insider, what constitutes MNPI, and sets forth the penalties for violations.

SEBI's Approach to Insider Trading:

SEBI is empowered to investigate insider trading cases by monitoring trade activity and suspicious transactions. It uses advanced surveillance systems like the **Integrated Market Surveillance System (IMSS)** and **Trade Analysis Software (TAS)** to track unusual trading patterns and detect potential violations. SEBI also collaborates with international bodies like the **U.S. SEC** and **FCA** in the U.K. to ensure cross-border compliance.

One of SEBI's landmark cases includes the **SEBI vs. Rakesh Agarwal** case, where the board prosecuted an insider for trading based on MNPI before an acquisition announcement. The judgment set a strong precedent for future insider trading cases in India.

SEC: Securities and Exchange Commission (U.S.)

The **Securities and Exchange Commission (SEC)** is the foremost regulatory authority in the United States, responsible for enforcing federal securities laws, regulating the securities industry, and protecting investors from fraudulent and manipulative practices. Established by the **Securities Exchange Act of 1934** in response to the **1929 stock market crash**, the SEC is a critical institution in maintaining the integrity of U.S. financial markets.

Key Roles of the SEC:

- **Enforcing securities laws**: The SEC enforces laws against market manipulation, insider trading, and other securities fraud.

- **Monitoring disclosures**: Public companies are required to file detailed financial reports (e.g., Form 10-Q, Form 10-K), which the SEC reviews to ensure full transparency.
- **Investigating insider trading**: The SEC conducts investigations into potential insider trading activities, often leading to civil penalties or criminal prosecution in coordination with the **Department of Justice (DOJ)**.

SEC's Tools for Preventing Insider Trading:

The SEC employs several tools and regulations to combat insider trading:

- **Rule 10b-5**: Enacted under the **Securities Exchange Act of 1934**, Rule 10b-5 is the primary legal tool used by the SEC to prosecute insider trading. This rule prohibits fraud and deceit in connection with the purchase or sale of securities.
- **MIDAS (Market Information Data Analytics System)**: The SEC's MIDAS system collects and analyzes billions of trade records, enabling the commission to detect suspicious trading patterns that could signal insider trading.

A landmark case under the SEC's jurisdiction was the **U.S. vs. Rajat Gupta**, where Gupta, a former Goldman Sachs board member, was convicted of insider trading for sharing confidential corporate information with hedge fund manager Raj Rajaratnam.

FCA: Financial Conduct Authority (UK)

The **Financial Conduct Authority (FCA)** is the United Kingdom's regulatory body responsible for overseeing the conduct of financial markets, ensuring market integrity, and protecting investors. Operating under the **Financial Services and Markets Act 2000 (FSMA)**, the FCA enforces the **Market Abuse Regulation (MAR)**, which includes strict rules on insider trading and market manipulation.

Key Functions of the FCA:

- **Market conduct rules**: The FCA enforces rules that aim to prevent market abuse, including insider trading and unlawful disclosure of inside information.

- **Supervising financial firms**: The FCA ensures that firms adhere to regulations that protect market integrity and investor interests.

- **Cross-border collaboration**: The FCA works closely with regulators like the **SEC** and **SEBI** to monitor and enforce insider trading laws internationally.

Insider Trading Regulations:

The **Market Abuse Regulation (MAR)**, introduced in 2016, is the cornerstone of the FCA's market abuse framework. It includes detailed provisions on:

- **Insider dealing**: Trading based on MNPI.

- **Unlawful disclosure of MNPI**: Sharing insider information that influences market prices.

The FCA's surveillance systems are equipped with advanced analytics that allow for the identification of suspicious trades, such as **unexplained spikes in volume or unusual price movements** prior to major corporate announcements.

IPO: Initial Public Offering

An **Initial Public Offering (IPO)** occurs when a privately held company offers shares to the public for the first time, transitioning from a privately held entity to a publicly traded one. IPOs are crucial to corporate growth as they allow companies to raise significant capital. However, IPOs are also highly regulated to ensure **fairness** and **transparency**.

Insider Trading in IPOs:

One of the critical areas for insider trading during IPOs involves insiders who have access to the company's non-public financial data, business projections, or information about the IPO pricing before it is disclosed to the public.

- In India, **SEBI's Prohibition of Insider Trading Regulations (2015)** covers trading during IPOs and pre-IPO communications.

- In the U.S., the SEC ensures that insiders, including underwriters, are restricted from trading based on non-public information related to an IPO.

For example, in the **Facebook IPO** case, the SEC fined underwriters who disclosed selective financial forecasts to preferred clients, leading to significant price volatility post-IPO.

TAS: Trade Analysis Software for Regulatory Surveillance

Trade Analysis Software (TAS) is an advanced tool used by regulators like SEBI and the SEC to identify abnormal trading patterns that could indicate **insider trading** or **market**

manipulation. TAS operates by analysing millions of trades in real-time, flagging suspicious activities for further investigation.

Key Features of TAS:

- **Pattern recognition**: TAS uses algorithms and machine learning to identify irregularities in trading volumes, price movements, and order types.

- **Cross-market analysis**: It can track trades across multiple markets, linking them to significant corporate events.

- **Data mining**: TAS analyses historical data and compares it with current trading patterns to detect deviations.

TAS is a critical component of SEBI's **Integrated Market Surveillance System (IMSS)**, which enhances SEBI's ability to monitor insider trading activities across Indian stock exchanges.

IMSS: Integrated Market Surveillance System

The **Integrated Market Surveillance System (IMSS)** is SEBI's proprietary system designed to detect and investigate **insider trading**, **market manipulation**, and other forms of securities fraud. It consolidates real-time data from the **NSE**, **BSE**, and other markets to monitor for irregular trading activity.

How IMSS Works:

- **Real-time data monitoring**: IMSS continuously tracks trading activity across markets, looking for unusual spikes in trading volume or price movements that coincide with corporate events.

- **Automated alerts**: The system flags suspicious trades and generates automated alerts for SEBI investigators.
- **Cross-border monitoring**: IMSS is capable of collaborating with international surveillance systems, allowing SEBI to track trades by foreign institutional investors (FIIs).

IMSS has become one of SEBI's most effective tools in investigating insider trading, enabling the regulator to respond swiftly and decisively when violations are detected.

Chapter 1

Insider Trading: A Critical Analysis

The Definition and Evolution of Insider Trading: An Advanced Legal and Financial Perspective

Insider trading, in its most sophisticated sense, refers to the **exploitation of material, non-public information (MNPI)** by corporate insiders, market professionals, or connected individuals to execute trades that affect market integrity. It is more than a violation of fiduciary duties—it strikes at the very core of **market transparency**, **regulatory compliance**, and **financial ethics**.

The evolution of insider trading law has been driven by the increasing complexity of financial instruments and the globalized nature of modern markets. In its nascent stages, particularly before the establishment of formal securities laws in the early 20th century, **insider trading was not universally recognized as unethical or illegal**. Wealthy investors, corporate executives, and key stakeholders routinely leveraged private knowledge to enrich themselves with minimal legal repercussions.

1930s: The U.S. Leads Regulatory Transformation

The watershed moment came with the **1934 Securities Exchange Act** following the 1929 Wall Street Crash, which exposed large-scale market manipulation by insiders. The introduction of **Rule 10b-5** under this Act marked the beginning of stringent insider trading regulations in the United States, establishing that trading on non-public information was not only unethical but a **serious federal crime**. The **SEC (Securities and Exchange Commission)**, with Rule 10b-5, built the foundations of modern insider trading enforcement, laying out that **"any manipulative, deceptive device or contrivance"** in securities trading would fall under its jurisdiction.

In subsequent decades, U.S. case law, such as **Chiarella v. United States** (1980) and **Dirks v. SEC** (1983), played a pivotal role in refining the legal interpretation of insider trading, especially concerning **tipper-tippee liability** and the fiduciary duty principle. These landmark cases shaped the modern insider trading landscape by clarifying that **individuals without a direct fiduciary relationship to the company** could still be culpable if they knowingly received insider information and traded on it.

The Global Context and Evolution

In contrast to the U.S., other jurisdictions, such as India and Europe, were slower in criminalizing insider trading. In India, while **SEBI (Securities and Exchange Board of India)** was established in 1988, its regulatory framework concerning insider trading matured significantly with the **Prohibition of Insider Trading Regulations, 1992**, and later, the **2015 update**, which aligned more closely with international standards.

In Europe, the **Market Abuse Directive (MAD)** and its successor, the **Market Abuse Regulation (MAR)**, provided a unified framework for the European Union, focusing on combating insider trading and market manipulation across member states. MAR, introduced in 2016, ensures that financial regulations across the EU are harmonized, reflecting a more robust and sophisticated approach to handling insider dealing across jurisdictions.

Internationally, countries such as **Singapore, Hong Kong**, and **Australia** have implemented **highly specialized regulations** that respond to their unique market structures while aligning with the broader regulatory frameworks seen in Western economies. The rise of **cross-border trading, multi-market transactions**, and **digital assets** has pushed regulators globally to adopt technologies such as **big data analytics, machine learning algorithms**, and **blockchain** to detect sophisticated insider trading schemes that are increasingly elusive.

The Strategic Importance of Transparency in Financial Markets

At the heart of any functioning financial system is the concept of information parity, where all market participants—whether institutional investors or retail traders—have equal access to public information. This ideal is central to the **Efficient Market Hypothesis (EMH)**, which asserts that asset prices fully reflect all available information.

Insider trading fundamentally disrupts this **equilibrium** by creating **informational asymmetry**: an uneven distribution of critical market knowledge. When insiders leverage non-public information to gain unfair advantages, it distorts the market's

price discovery mechanism, leading to inaccurate asset valuations and misallocated capital.

In technical terms, insider trading subverts the principles of **market liquidity** and **order execution**. A market distorted by insiders behaves inefficiently, where trading volume and price volatility no longer reflect the natural supply-demand dynamic but rather the clandestine activities of privileged individuals. For example:

- **Liquidity imbalances** occur when insiders offload large quantities of shares ahead of a negative announcement, creating artificial sell pressure.
- **Price gapping** results when insiders trade on MNPI, causing sharp, unexplained movements in stock prices, especially in thinly traded or illiquid markets.

Information Symmetry and Market Depth

In modern financial markets, **market depth**—the ability to absorb large orders without significant price changes—relies on the assumption that all market participants are operating on the same level of information. When insider trading occurs, it disrupts market depth, leading to **spikes in volatility** and **disruptions in bid-ask spreads**. These disruptions erode investor confidence, causing **institutional players** to widen spreads or reduce exposure, further weakening market stability.

The manipulation of **order books** by insiders, particularly in **High-Frequency Trading (HFT)** environments, can compound these effects. HFT systems react to **microsecond changes** in market conditions, and when insiders place trades based on MNPI, these systems can amplify the impact of their trades, leading to **flash crashes** or other market anomalies.

Quantitative Finance: The Invisible Hand of Insider Trading

In an increasingly quantitative financial landscape, insider trading's impact is often concealed by the sheer complexity of algorithms and trading platforms. Sophisticated **quantitative traders** and **hedge funds** that rely on **predictive models** are particularly vulnerable to the effects of insider trading, as it distorts the patterns they seek to exploit. The misuse of MNPI can skew predictive models, leading to inaccurate algorithmic trading strategies that result in **unintended losses**.

Transparency is, therefore, not only a legal or ethical issue but also a **technical imperative** for maintaining the viability of complex, data-driven trading strategies. Ensuring that insiders do not undermine these mechanisms is a top priority for **compliance officers**, **financial engineers**, and **regulators** alike.

Global Regulatory Responses to Insider Trading: A Sophisticated Enforcement Ecosystem

The international response to insider trading has grown increasingly sophisticated, with regulators deploying cutting-edge technologies, multi-jurisdictional cooperation, and **automated surveillance** systems. Regulatory bodies are now working beyond mere legal frameworks, incorporating **AI-Powered Surveillance Tools (APST)** and **Data Analytics Platforms (DAP)** to detect and investigate suspicious market activities.

1. **SEC's MIDAS**: The **Market Information Data Analytics System (MIDAS)** is an advanced tool used by the SEC to capture and analyse millions of trades per day in real time. MIDAS processes vast datasets of **quote-level data**, identifying abnormal trading patterns,

such as **spikes in trading volume, unusual timing of trades,** and **specific trading behaviours tied to corporate events**. The system can recognize subtle patterns that human investigators might miss, helping the SEC pinpoint instances of insider trading.

2. **SEBI's IMSS and Big Data Analytics**: In India, SEBI has implemented the **Integrated Market Surveillance System (IMSS)**, designed to track large volumes of transactions across multiple stock exchanges. By leveraging **big data analytics**, SEBI can monitor cross-market trades and detect insider activities that may otherwise go unnoticed. This system complements SEBI's broader regulatory strategy, which emphasizes **real-time surveillance** and **data-driven enforcement**.

3. **FCA's MAR Compliance Framework**: The **Financial Conduct Authority (FCA)** in the UK uses the **Market Abuse Regulation (MAR)** framework to enforce strict controls over insider trading. The FCA's system integrates **cross-border data sharing**, particularly with European regulators, ensuring that trades executed across different financial hubs do not escape scrutiny. **Collaborative platforms** like **ESMA (European Securities and Markets Authority)** facilitate this seamless monitoring, strengthening the FCA's ability to combat market abuse.

International Cooperation: The Global Fight Against Insider Trading

In an era where financial markets are interconnected, insider trading is no longer a domestic issue but a global one.

Cross-border cooperation among regulatory bodies has become crucial in combating insider trading, as many schemes involve actors in multiple jurisdictions. The **International Organization of Securities Commissions (IOSCO)** plays a pivotal role in facilitating global coordination by establishing **memoranda of understanding (MOUs)** between regulators. This ensures the seamless exchange of data and information, particularly for multi-market trades.

For example, a multinational corporation with insider information on an upcoming merger may trade its stocks in several countries, including the U.S., India, and Europe. Without international cooperation, it would be nearly impossible to detect the full scope of this illicit activity. However, through coordinated efforts, such as the **SEBI-SEC MOU**, regulators can track trades across multiple jurisdictions and share key insights in real-time, leading to more efficient investigations and prosecutions.

How Insider Trading Erodes Investor Confidence and Market Integrity

Insider trading not only distorts market fairness but also has profound effects on **investor confidence**, a critical component of market liquidity and corporate valuation. Investors, both retail and institutional, expect a certain level of **fiduciary duty** and **equitable access to information**. When insiders use their privileged position to exploit MNPI, the market becomes a less attractive venue for legitimate investments.

Impact on Institutional and Retail Investors

Institutional investors—such as pension funds, mutual funds, and sovereign wealth funds—rely on **reliable, transparent**

markets for effective portfolio management. The presence of insider trading introduces an element of unpredictability that undermines their **quantitative models** and **investment strategies**, forcing them to adopt a more conservative approach to capital allocation. This can result in higher **liquidity premiums**, reduced **market participation**, and, ultimately, less efficient capital flows.

Retail investors, on the other hand, are even more vulnerable to the effects of insider trading. Unlike institutional investors, they lack the advanced tools and strategies necessary to navigate a manipulated market. As a result, insider trading diminishes retail participation and weakens the market's overall liquidity.

Long-Term Consequences on Market Integrity

The longer-term consequences of insider trading extend far beyond individual losses or gains. When insider trading becomes systemic, it has the potential to **de-legitimize entire markets**, leading to **capital flight**, reduced foreign direct investment (FDI), and negative impacts on **national economic growth**. Market integrity is a fragile construct that requires continuous monitoring and enforcement to sustain investor trust.

Global markets depend on the perception of fairness and transparency. Repeated insider trading violations, especially those involving major corporations, send a signal to investors that the market is inherently skewed in Favor of insiders. This, in turn, can trigger a **self-reinforcing feedback loop**, where diminished trust leads to reduced liquidity, which exacerbates market inefficiencies and increases **systemic risk**.

Chapter 2

The Role and Importance of Stock Markets

Stock Markets as the Engines of Economic Growth

Stock markets are not just trading platforms; they are the **financial arteries** that drive economic expansion, innovation, and global integration. By facilitating the **allocation of capital** to its most productive uses, stock markets provide businesses with the financial resources needed to fund innovation, create jobs, and contribute to national economic growth.

At the core of stock markets is their role in **capital formation**, where companies raise funds by issuing shares (equity financing) or bonds (debt financing). This capital is crucial for businesses looking to scale, innovate, or expand into new markets. Stock markets, through **Initial Public Offerings (IPOs)**, allow companies to transition from private ownership to public ownership, enabling them to tap into a broader pool of investors. The funds raised through these IPOs are used for **research and development (R&D), mergers and acquisitions (M&A)**, and **infrastructure development**.

Mechanics of Capital Formation

1. **Equity Financing**: Companies issue shares to the public, granting investors partial ownership in return for capital. This process injects liquidity into the company without increasing debt obligations. In return, investors receive the potential for dividends and **capital gains** as the company grows.

2. **Debt Financing**: Companies can also issue corporate bonds, allowing them to raise capital while maintaining ownership control. These bonds provide investors with regular interest payments, known as the **coupon rate**, and the principal is repaid at maturity. The balance between equity and debt issuance is crucial for maintaining a company's financial stability and **cost of capital**.

Stock exchanges such as the **New York Stock Exchange (NYSE), NASDAQ, National Stock Exchange of India (NSE)**, and **Bombay Stock Exchange (BSE)** are global financial hubs that allow for the smooth functioning of these capital-raising activities. The sheer size and scale of these exchanges, with market capitalizations reaching **trillions of dollars**, reflect the depth and breadth of the economies they serve.

Economic Multiplier Effect of Stock Markets

The **multiplier effect** generated by stock markets is profound:

1. **Job Creation**: Companies use the capital raised from public offerings to invest in expansion, which often leads to job creation. This includes hiring for new

factories, expanding product lines, and developing new technologies.

2. **Technological Innovation**: With access to fresh capital, companies can increase their R&D budgets, leading to innovations that drive productivity. For example, **Tesla**, after its IPO in 2010, leveraged capital to develop its electric vehicle technology, revolutionizing the automotive industry.

3. **Infrastructure and National Growth**: Large-scale infrastructure projects are often funded through public capital raised via stock markets. For instance, real estate giants or energy companies often raise capital for large construction projects, fueling growth in associated sectors such as materials, construction, and labor markets.

Efficient Market Hypothesis (EMH) vs. Real-World Trading: Market Anomalies

The **Efficient Market Hypothesis (EMH)** is a foundational theory in financial economics, asserting that financial markets are "informationally efficient," meaning that stock prices fully reflect all available information at any given time. This hypothesis, championed by **Eugene Fama** in the 1960s, is built on the assumption that **investors are rational**, and that market prices are adjusted instantaneously to reflect new data. According to EMH, it is impossible to consistently achieve returns that exceed the market average without taking on additional risk.

Forms of Market Efficiency:

1. **Weak Form Efficiency**: In weak form efficiency, all **historical price data** is already reflected in stock prices, implying that technical analysis (analyzing past price movements and volume data) cannot yield consistent excess returns.

2. **Semi-Strong Form Efficiency**: In semi-strong form efficiency, stock prices reflect all **publicly available information**, including financial statements, earnings reports, macroeconomic factors, and corporate announcements. Investors cannot consistently achieve excess returns by analyzing this public information.

3. **Strong Form Efficiency**: The strong form of EMH suggests that stock prices reflect all information, both **public and private** (MNPI), meaning that even insiders with access to private information cannot consistently earn abnormal returns.

While EMH is a powerful theoretical construct, empirical evidence from real-world trading frequently challenges its validity. **Market anomalies**, driven by **behavioural finance**, **information asymmetry**, and **market inefficiencies**, suggest that prices do not always reflect all available information, and that irrational investor behaviour can result in **mispricing**.

Key Market Anomalies That Contradict EMH:

1. **Momentum Anomaly**: The momentum effect, where stocks that have performed well over a short period continue to outperform, contradicts the weak form of EMH. Research has shown that portfolios of momentum stocks have generated higher-than-average

returns, particularly in the short term. This anomaly suggests that prices adjust slowly, providing an opportunity for traders to exploit.

2. **Value Anomaly**: Stocks with low **price-to-earnings (P/E) ratios** or high **book-to-market ratios** tend to outperform those with higher ratios. This value anomaly contradicts the semi-strong form of EMH. The success of **value investing**, popularized by **Benjamin Graham** and **Warren Buffett**, demonstrates that undervalued companies can provide **long-term returns** that exceed the market average.

3. **Small-Cap Effect**: Small-cap stocks often outperform their large-cap counterparts over long periods. This is partly due to **liquidity constraints** and the fact that small-cap stocks tend to be under-researched by institutional investors. This anomaly suggests that there is **inefficient pricing** in smaller, less-liquid markets, providing opportunities for superior returns.

4. **Calendar Effects**: The **January Effect**, where stock prices, particularly small-cap stocks, tend to rise more in January than in other months, and the **Weekend Effect**, where prices tend to fall on Mondays, contradict the idea of an efficient market where prices should not be influenced by calendar cycles.

Behavioural Finance and Market Inefficiencies

While EMH assumes that investors are rational, **behavioural finance** provides evidence that market participants often act irrationally due to cognitive biases. Common biases include:

1. **Overconfidence Bias**: Traders may overestimate their ability to predict market movements based on their personal analysis, leading to excessive risk-taking.
2. **Loss Aversion**: Investors are more sensitive to losses than gains, which can result in **irrational selling** during market downturns or holding onto losing positions in the hope of a rebound.
3. **Herding Behaviour**: Investors tend to follow the crowd, which can amplify **market bubbles** or **panic selling** during crashes.

These behavioural factors lead to inefficiencies in pricing and present opportunities for savvy investors to exploit market anomalies, thus challenging the EMH.

Capital Formation and Liquidity in Global Exchanges: NSE, BSE, NYSE, and NASDAQ

Capital formation and **liquidity** are the twin pillars of functioning stock markets. Capital formation refers to the ability of firms to raise long-term financing through the sale of equity or debt, while liquidity is the measure of how quickly and efficiently assets can be bought or sold without impacting their price.

The Primary Market and Capital Formation

In the **primary market**, companies issue new securities to the public to raise capital. This process is particularly vital during **Initial Public Offerings (IPOs)**, where a private company sells its shares to the public for the first time. Successful capital formation depends on the company's ability to attract investors through **sound financials**, **growth potential**, and **strong corporate governance**.

Global stock exchanges such as **NYSE, NASDAQ, NSE,** and **BSE** have become central to global capital formation. In 2021 alone, IPOs raised approximately **$301 billion globally**, with **U.S. exchanges accounting for 60%** of that total. In India, the NSE and BSE have attracted large-scale IPOs from companies in the technology and financial sectors, raising billions of dollars in capital.

For instance:

1. **Reliance Industries** and **Tata Consultancy Services (TCS)**, two of India's largest corporations, raised significant capital through public listings on the BSE and NSE, fuelling their expansion into global markets.
2. **Alibaba's 2014 IPO** on the NYSE raised **$25 billion**, the largest IPO in history at the time, showcasing the importance of global capital markets in financing corporate expansion.

The Secondary Market and Liquidity

Once shares are issued in the primary market, they are actively traded in the **secondary market**. The liquidity of these shares—how easily they can be bought or sold without affecting the price—depends on market depth, participant diversity, and regulatory safeguards.

Liquidity in stock markets is enhanced through several mechanisms:

1. **Market Makers**: Designated market makers (DMMs) and specialists provide continuous quotes for buying

and selling shares, ensuring smooth market operations, particularly during volatile periods.

2. **Electronic Trading**: Global exchanges, such as NASDAQ and the NSE, rely on **high-frequency trading (HFT)** systems and advanced **algorithmic trading** to provide continuous liquidity, enabling the rapid execution of large-volume trades.

3. **Bid-Ask Spreads**: The **spread** between the bid (buy) and ask (sell) prices is a crucial indicator of liquidity. Narrow bid-ask spreads reflect high liquidity and low transaction costs, while wider spreads signal lower liquidity, where buying or selling large volumes may significantly impact the price.

The importance of liquidity can be seen in **volatile market environments**, where sudden **market corrections** or **crashes** expose the fragility of less liquid stocks. High liquidity provides a buffer during turbulent times, allowing investors to exit positions with minimal losses, thus preserving market stability.

Global Exchanges as Liquidity Providers

1. **NYSE**: As the world's largest exchange by market capitalization, the NYSE facilitates deep liquidity, with an **average daily trading volume exceeding 2.4 billion shares**. Its sophisticated trading infrastructure ensures price stability, even during periods of high volatility.

2. **NASDAQ**: Known for its focus on technology stocks, NASDAQ offers deep liquidity for tech giants like **Apple, Amazon**, and **Tesla**, which see significant daily trading volumes, ensuring tight spreads and minimal price impact.

3. **NSE and BSE**: In India, the **NSE** has gained prominence over the BSE in terms of liquidity, with the **Nifty 50** serving as a benchmark index for investors seeking exposure to India's economic growth. The NSE's advanced **electronic trading system** provides liquidity to domestic and foreign investors alike.

How Insider Trading Distorts Price Discovery and Market Efficiency

Price discovery—the process by which market prices adjust to new information—lies at the heart of **market efficiency**. Insider trading severely disrupts this process by creating **information asymmetry** between insiders with access to **MNPI** and the rest of the market participants.

In a fair and efficient market, all relevant public information is factored into asset prices, allowing prices to accurately reflect the intrinsic value of a security. However, insider trading gives certain individuals the ability to act on non-public information, such as **pending earnings announcements**, **mergers**, or **regulatory approvals**, leading to mispriced securities.

Key Mechanisms by Which Insider Trading Distorts Markets:

1. **Information Asymmetry and Adverse Selection**: In the presence of insider trading, **adverse selection** occurs. Insiders trade based on superior information, creating a market where informed participants profit at the expense of uninformed traders. This leads to higher transaction costs for the average investor, as liquidity providers demand higher **liquidity premiums** to account for the risk of trading against insiders.

2. **Volatility and Noise Trading**: Insider trading often precedes major corporate announcements, resulting in **abnormal price volatility**. This volatility, which is often amplified by **high-frequency trading (HFT)** systems, creates **noise** that makes it difficult for legitimate traders to interpret price movements. When insiders trade heavily based on MNPI, it injects artificial volatility into the market, distorting natural price discovery.

3. **Market Manipulation**: In markets susceptible to insider trading, insiders may engage in **pump-and-dump schemes**, where they artificially inflate the price of a stock by disseminating false information or trading heavily to create buying pressure. Once the price rises, they sell off their holdings, leaving ordinary investors with significant losses. These practices not only distort price discovery but also erode trust in the fairness of the market.

Empirical Evidence of Insider Trading's Impact:

Numerous studies have shown that insider trading leads to **mispriced assets** and **increased risk premiums**. For example, a study by **Bhattacharya and Daouk (2002)** found that markets with strong insider trading enforcement tend to have **lower costs of capital**, while those with weak enforcement experience **higher equity risk premiums**, reflecting the inherent risk of trading in manipulated markets.

Conclusion

Stock markets are the engines of economic growth, facilitating capital formation, liquidity, and efficient price discovery. However, insider trading presents a significant threat to market integrity by distorting the price discovery process and undermining investor confidence. By leveraging advanced regulatory frameworks, enhanced surveillance mechanisms, and sophisticated trading platforms, global markets can mitigate the detrimental effects of insider trading and maintain their role as engines of economic growth and innovation.

Through the continuous development of **market regulations**, **cross-border collaboration**, and **technological advancements**, stock markets can evolve to combat the challenges posed by insider trading while maintaining **market efficiency** and **investor trust**.

Chapter 3

The Key Mechanisms of Stock Market Operations

Understanding Securities, Equities, Bonds, and Derivatives: A Holistic View

At the foundation of any stock market are **securities**, which serve as the primary instruments through which capital is raised, risk is hedged, and investments are made. To fully appreciate the complexity of stock market operations, one must first understand the types of securities traded—**equities, bonds, and derivatives**—and how they function in the market's broader ecosystem.

Equities (Common Stock)

Equities, often referred to as common stock, represent ownership in a corporation. As equity holders, investors gain **voting rights** in company decisions, a share of the company's **profits** through dividends, and the potential for capital appreciation as the company's value increases. Equities are among the most actively traded securities in stock markets and serve as a barometer of economic sentiment and corporate health.

- **Capital Appreciation**: Equities are primarily valued for their potential to generate **capital gains**—the increase in the value of the stock over time. Investors buy equities at current market prices, expecting the company's future performance to boost the share price.

- **Dividend Income**: Some companies return profits to shareholders through dividends, providing a regular income stream. Dividend yield—calculated as **annual dividends per share divided by stock price**—is a key metric used by investors to assess the income potential of a stock.

- **Risk and Volatility**: Equities are inherently more volatile than other financial instruments such as bonds. Investors face the risk of **price fluctuations**, driven by changes in earnings, market sentiment, macroeconomic conditions, and company-specific events like **mergers and acquisitions** or **leadership changes**. Tools like the **Capital Asset Pricing Model (CAPM)** and **beta** (a measure of volatility relative to the market) are essential for assessing equity risk.

Bonds

Bonds are debt securities issued by governments, municipalities, or corporations. Investors who purchase bonds are effectively lending money to the issuer in exchange for periodic **interest payments** (coupons) and the return of the principal amount at maturity. Bonds are considered safer than equities, but they also come with their own set of risks—**interest rate risk**, **credit risk**, and **inflation risk**.

- **Government Bonds**: Issued by sovereign entities, government bonds, such as **U.S. Treasuries**, are typically seen as risk-free or low-risk instruments. They play a vital role in portfolio diversification and are often used as a benchmark for risk-free rates.

- **Corporate Bonds**: Corporations issue bonds to finance expansion, acquisitions, or day-to-day operations. **Investment-grade bonds** are issued by financially stable companies, while **high-yield bonds** (junk bonds) are riskier but offer higher yields to compensate for default risk.

- **Yield Curves and Interest Rates**: Bonds are sensitive to changes in interest rates, reflected in the **yield curve**—a graphical representation of bond yields across different maturities. An **inverted yield curve**, where short-term yields exceed long-term yields, is often seen as a signal of an impending economic recession.

Derivatives

Derivatives are complex financial instruments whose value is derived from an underlying asset or benchmark. Common types include **futures, options, swaps**, and **forwards**. Derivatives are used for **hedging, speculation**, and **arbitrage**, enabling market participants to manage risk or leverage their positions.

- **Options**: Options provide the holder with the right, but not the obligation, to buy or sell an asset at a predetermined price within a specified time. The two main types of options are **call options** (buy) and **put**

options (sell). Options pricing is determined by factors such as **volatility** (calculated using models like the **Black-Scholes model**) and time decay.

- **Futures**: Futures contracts obligate parties to buy or sell an asset at a set price on a future date. These are primarily used by institutional players to hedge against price fluctuations in commodities, currencies, or financial indices.

- **Swaps and Forwards**: In **interest rate swaps**, for example, two parties exchange cash flows—one receiving a fixed rate while the other receives a floating rate. **Currency swaps** are used to hedge foreign exchange risk. **Forwards**, similar to futures, are over-the-counter contracts that allow parties to buy or sell an asset at a future date, customized to meet specific needs.

Securities Market Structure

Securities markets are split into two main segments:

- **Primary Market**: The market where new securities are issued and sold to the public. This is where companies raise new capital through **Initial Public Offerings (IPOs)**, bond issues, and other methods.

- **Secondary Market**: Once securities have been issued, they are traded on the secondary market, where price discovery and liquidity occur. The secondary market allows for the transfer of ownership between investors, providing essential liquidity to the financial system.

Market Indices: How Sensex, Nifty, S&P 500, and FTSE Reflect Economic Health

Market indices are crucial tools for evaluating the overall performance of a stock market or a specific segment of the economy. These indices aggregate the prices of selected stocks, providing a benchmark that reflects market sentiment, economic strength, and the financial health of the companies they represent.

Sensex and Nifty (India)

- **Sensex (Bombay Stock Exchange, BSE)**: The **Sensex**, or the **BSE 30**, is an index that tracks the performance of the top 30 companies listed on the **Bombay Stock Exchange** based on market capitalization and liquidity. The companies in the Sensex are representative of India's key sectors, such as banking, technology, energy, and pharmaceuticals. The movement of the Sensex serves as a **barometer of investor confidence** and economic activity in India.

- **Nifty 50 (National Stock Exchange, NSE)**: The **Nifty 50** is the flagship index of the **National Stock Exchange (NSE)** and comprises the 50 largest companies listed on the exchange. Companies in the Nifty 50 are market leaders in sectors such as IT, banking, and consumer goods, making the Nifty a comprehensive reflection of India's economy.

S&P 500 (U.S.)

The **S&P 500** is one of the most important stock market indices globally, tracking the performance of 500 of the largest companies listed on U.S. exchanges by market capitalization. As a **market-cap-weighted index**, companies like **Apple, Microsoft, Amazon**, and **Tesla** have a significant impact on the index's overall performance. The S&P 500 is often used as a proxy for the **health of the U.S. economy** and is a benchmark for institutional investors globally.

FTSE 100 (U.K.)

The **FTSE 100** index tracks the 100 largest companies by market capitalization listed on the **London Stock Exchange (LSE)**. The companies included in the FTSE 100 are multinational corporations from industries such as financial services, mining, energy, and consumer goods. This index is closely watched as a measure of the **economic health of the U.K.**, reflecting both domestic and international business conditions.

Key Roles of Market Indices:

- **Economic Indicators**: Rising indices are typically associated with **economic growth**, increasing investor confidence, and corporate profitability, while falling indices may signal **economic contraction**, uncertainty, or declining investor sentiment.

- **Benchmarking**: Institutional investors and asset managers use indices to benchmark the performance of mutual funds, exchange-traded funds (ETFs), and pension funds. For example, a fund that tracks the **S&P 500** is expected to generate returns in line with the index.

- **Risk Management**: Market indices serve as the foundation for various derivative instruments, including **index futures** and **options**. Traders use these derivatives to hedge against market volatility or speculate on market movements. For instance, **S&P 500 index futures** allow institutional traders to hedge their portfolios against large price swings.

Regulatory Bodies Across the Globe: SEBI, SEC, FCA, and ESMA

Stock market operations are tightly regulated by agencies that enforce compliance, protect investors, and ensure market stability. Global regulators aim to mitigate risks such as **insider trading**, **market manipulation**, and **corporate fraud**, ensuring that markets operate transparently and efficiently.

Securities and Exchange Board of India (SEBI)

SEBI is the principal regulatory body overseeing the securities markets in India. It was established in 1988 and granted statutory powers in 1992 through the **SEBI Act**. SEBI's responsibilities include:

- Regulating and supervising stock exchanges to ensure fair trading practices.

- Enforcing the Prohibition of Insider Trading Regulations (2015) to prevent the misuse of Material Non-Public Information (MNPI).

- Monitoring corporate governance practices, ensuring transparency in public companies.

SEBI's use of cutting-edge tools such as the **Integrated Market Surveillance System (IMSS)** enables the regulator to monitor market activity in real-time, identifying patterns that could indicate illegal activity or **market manipulation**.

Securities and Exchange Commission (SEC, U.S.)

The SEC is the regulatory authority responsible for enforcing federal securities laws in the United States. Established by the **Securities Exchange Act of 1934**, the SEC plays a critical role in ensuring market integrity and investor protection.

Key areas of focus include:

- Regulating securities exchanges such as the NYSE and NASDAQ.

- Enforcing anti-fraud regulations, particularly Rule 10b-5, which governs insider trading and market manipulation.

- Ensuring corporate transparency through required filings like Form 10-K (annual reports) and Form 4 (insider trading disclosures).

Financial Conduct Authority (FCA, U.K.)

The **Financial Conduct Authority (FCA)** regulates financial markets in the U.K. under the **Financial Services and Markets Act 2000**. The FCA's role includes:

- **Supervising market conduct**, ensuring that trading activities comply with the **Market Abuse Regulation (MAR).**

- **Investigating market abuses** such as insider trading, front-running, and wash trades.

- **Cooperating with international regulators**, including the SEC and ESMA, to ensure consistent enforcement of financial regulations across borders.

European Securities and Markets Authority (ESMA)

ESMA is a European Union agency responsible for overseeing financial markets across member states. ESMA's role is critical in harmonizing regulations across Europe, particularly through the enforcement of the **Market Abuse Regulation (MAR)** and **MiFID II**. ESMA focuses on:

- **Regulating cross-border securities trading**, ensuring that national regulators implement EU-wide rules consistently.

- **Enhancing transparency** through corporate reporting standards and preventing market manipulation and insider trading.

How Stock Market Intermediaries Work: Brokers, Market Makers, and Clearing Houses

Stock market operations rely on a network of intermediaries that facilitate the smooth execution of trades, provide liquidity, and ensure that transactions are settled promptly. These intermediaries—**brokers**, **market makers**, and **clearing houses**—play a pivotal role in maintaining market stability and liquidity.

Brokers

Brokers are intermediaries who execute buy and sell orders on behalf of clients. Brokers can be divided into two main categories:

- **Full-Service Brokers**: Provide personalized services, including investment advice, research, and wealth management. Examples include **Goldman Sachs** and **Merrill Lynch**.

- **Discount Brokers**: Offer basic trade execution services at lower costs. Discount brokers like **Robinhood** and **Interactive Brokers** have gained popularity among retail investors for their commission-free trading platforms.

Market Makers

Market makers are essential for ensuring liquidity in the markets by continuously quoting buy and sell prices (bid-ask spreads) for specific securities. Their role is to facilitate trades and reduce volatility by absorbing large buy and sell orders, especially during periods of market stress.

- **Designated Market Makers (DMMs)**: On exchanges like the NYSE, DMMs are responsible for ensuring a liquid and orderly market for specific stocks. They step in to provide liquidity when there is an imbalance between buy and sell orders, preventing excessive price swings.

Clearing Houses

Clearing houses serve as intermediaries that manage the settlement of trades, ensuring that securities and cash are exchanged between the buyer and seller after a trade is executed. Clearing houses also play a key role in mitigating counterparty risk by guaranteeing the completion of a trade, even if one party defaults.

- **Clearing and Settlement**: The clearing house ensures that the trade is settled on time, with securities being transferred to the buyer and cash to the seller. For example, in the U.S., the **Depository Trust & Clearing**

Corporation (DTCC) oversees the clearing and settlement of trades on major exchanges.

- **Risk Management**: Clearing houses impose **margin requirements** to protect against default risk, requiring market participants to post collateral before executing large trades. This helps ensure market stability and prevents systemic risks.

Conclusion

Stock markets are complex ecosystems driven by the interaction of diverse financial instruments, market indices, regulatory bodies, and intermediaries. The smooth functioning of these markets depends on the intricate mechanisms that facilitate capital formation, liquidity, and price discovery. Indices such as the **Sensex, Nifty, S&P 500**, and **FTSE** serve as barometers of economic performance, while regulatory authorities like SEBI, SEC, FCA, and ESMA ensure market integrity and protect investors from fraud and manipulation. Market intermediaries—brokers, market makers, and clearing houses—further ensure efficient trading, liquidity, and risk management, enabling markets to function as engines of economic growth and financial stability.

In this ever-evolving landscape, the efficient operation of stock markets requires not only a strong regulatory framework but also the seamless collaboration of all stakeholders to maintain transparency, fairness, and investor trust.

Chapter 4

Corporate Transparency and Financial Disclosure

Decoding Annual Reports: From Financial Statements to Management Disclosures

Annual reports serve as the **cornerstone of corporate transparency**, offering investors, regulators, and other stakeholders a detailed view of a company's financial health, operations, and future prospects. These reports provide critical data that allows market participants to make informed investment decisions. A robust understanding of **financial statements, management disclosures**, and **supplementary information** contained within these reports is essential for evaluating a company's performance and mitigating potential risks such as **insider trading**.

1. Financial Statements: The Heart of Corporate Transparency

Financial statements are the most scrutinized part of an annual report, as they present a company's financial health through standardized documents that adhere to **Generally**

Accepted Accounting Principles (GAAP) or **International Financial Reporting Standards (IFRS)**. They include the balance sheet, income statement, cash flow statement, and statement of changes in equity.

- **Balance Sheet**: Provides a snapshot of a company's assets, liabilities, and shareholders' equity at a specific point in time. Key metrics, such as the **current ratio** and **debt-to-equity ratio**, offer insights into the company's liquidity and financial leverage. A company with a high debt-to-equity ratio may face higher risk during economic downturns or rising interest rates, making it less attractive to risk-averse investors.

- Income Statement: Also known as the **Profit & Loss (P&L) statement**, this section shows revenues, expenses, and profits over a fiscal year. Investors typically focus on **earnings per share (EPS)**, **gross margins**, and **net income**, which help assess profitability trends. A rising EPS indicates strong profit growth, which can attract long-term institutional investors.

- Cash Flow Statement: Unlike the income statement, which reports earnings, the **cash flow statement** tracks actual cash inflows and outflows from operating, investing, and financing activities. **Free cash flow (FCF)**—the cash remaining after capital expenditures—can be a powerful metric for gauging a company's ability to reinvest in its operations or return value to shareholders through dividends or stock buybacks.

- **Statement of Changes in Equity**: Shows changes in a company's equity over the reporting period, including items like retained earnings and share repurchases. This statement helps investors understand how profits are being utilized, whether for dividends, debt reduction, or reinvestment.

2. Management Disclosures and Footnotes: Understanding Risks and Liabilities

Footnotes and **management disclosures** provide critical context to financial statements, highlighting any contingent liabilities, regulatory issues, or off-balance-sheet transactions. These sections are often scrutinized by institutional investors and analysts to uncover hidden risks that may not be immediately visible in the core financial data.

- **Contingent Liabilities**: These are potential liabilities that may arise depending on the outcome of future events, such as litigation or regulatory fines. For example, if a pharmaceutical company is facing lawsuits related to the safety of its drugs, contingent liabilities provide a measure of the potential financial risk involved.

- **Off-Balance-Sheet Items**: Some financial obligations, such as **operating leases** or **joint ventures**, may not be fully reflected on the balance sheet but can significantly impact a company's risk profile. Investors should scrutinize these items to ensure they understand the full extent of the company's financial commitments.

Management disclosures also highlight **Key Performance Indicators (KPIs)** and strategies. These forward-looking insights help investors gauge the company's potential growth trajectory, competitive positioning, and strategic initiatives. In particular, investors analyse **Return on Equity (ROE)**, **Return on Assets**

(ROA), and other KPIs to assess management's effectiveness in generating returns on shareholder capital.

Corporate Governance Reports and Their Role in Insider Trading Prevention

Corporate governance reports have evolved into powerful tools for enhancing **market transparency** and **mitigating the risk of insider trading**. These reports provide insights into the structure of a company's board, internal controls, and executive compensation—**all critical factors** in ensuring that corporate leaders act in the best interest of shareholders.

1. The Structure and Independence of the Board

A key element of corporate governance is the **board of directors**, which is responsible for overseeing management and ensuring the company's long-term success. Boards must include a mix of **executive directors** (senior company executives) and **independent directors**, who are not affiliated with the company or its management. Independent directors are particularly important for maintaining accountability and reducing the risk of **corporate malfeasance** or **insider trading**.

- **Independent Directors and Audit Committees**: Independent directors typically chair the **audit committee**, which is responsible for reviewing financial statements, overseeing external audits, and monitoring internal controls. An audit committee with robust oversight can help prevent financial irregularities that may create opportunities for **insider trading**. In India, under the **SEBI (Listing Obligations and Disclosure Requirements) Regulations**, audit committees must consist of at least two-thirds independent directors.

- **Board Diversity and Competence**: Research shows that diverse boards—composed of directors with varied expertise, backgrounds, and gender diversity—are more effective in **governance and risk management**. Companies with boards that include finance experts, legal professionals, and industry veterans are better equipped to navigate complex regulatory landscapes and prevent illegal activities like insider trading.

2. Executive Compensation and Insider Trading Risks

Executive compensation packages are often linked to stock performance, which can incentivize **unethical behaviour** if governance controls are weak. **Stock Options, Restricted Stock Units (RSUs),** and **Performance-Linked Bonuses** may encourage executives to engage in **insider trading** to manipulate stock prices and increase their personal wealth. To mitigate these risks, corporate governance reports should provide full transparency on executive compensation, including **clawback provisions** that allow companies to recover compensation in the event of misconduct.

- **Clawback Provisions**: These clauses ensure that companies can reclaim performance-based compensation if it is later discovered that the financial performance was artificially inflated due to misconduct, including insider trading.

- **Pre-clearance Policies**: Many companies implement **pre-clearance policies** requiring executives to obtain approval before trading company stock. This mitigates the risk of trading on **material non-public information (MNPI)** and aligns with the **Prohibition of Insider**

Trading Regulations (PITR) enforced by regulators like **SEBI** and the **SEC**.

The Role of Auditors and Independent Directors in Ensuring Transparency

Auditors, both internal and external, serve as the **first line of defense** in detecting and preventing financial fraud and **market manipulation**. They work in tandem with independent directors to ensure the accuracy and integrity of a company's financial statements, safeguarding shareholders and preventing **insider trading**.

1. External Auditors: Ensuring Compliance and Accuracy

External auditors provide an **objective assessment** of a company's financial statements and internal controls. By following established auditing standards (e.g., **International Standards on Auditing (ISA)**), external auditors evaluate whether the company's financial disclosures are free from material misstatement. These audits are critical in detecting **accounting irregularities**, which can signal potential insider trading or corporate fraud.

- **Audit Reports**: After completing their assessment, external auditors issue an **audit report**, stating whether the financial statements present a true and fair view of the company's financial position. A **qualified audit opinion**—indicating issues with the financial statements—can have severe consequences, including regulatory scrutiny and investor backlash.

- **Forensic Audits**: In cases where there is suspicion of financial fraud or insider trading, forensic audits are conducted to trace the flow of funds, uncover **red flags**, and identify fraudulent transactions. Forensic audits often use **data analytics** to detect anomalies in trading patterns or financial transactions that may indicate illegal activity.

2. Internal Auditors: Continuous Monitoring and Risk Management

Internal auditors are embedded within the organization and focus on evaluating the effectiveness of **internal controls** and **risk management systems**. Unlike external auditors, who conduct periodic audits, internal auditors perform ongoing assessments to identify potential vulnerabilities that could be exploited by insiders for financial gain.

- **Risk-Based Auditing**: Internal auditors often use **risk-based auditing** to prioritize their efforts on the most significant financial and operational risks. By focusing on areas prone to fraud or insider trading—such as revenue recognition, related-party transactions, or expense misreporting—internal auditors help strengthen the company's defense mechanisms against unethical behaviour.

3. Independent Directors: Governance Oversight

Independent directors play an essential role in overseeing the company's financial reporting and audit functions. In many jurisdictions, including India, **corporate governance codes** require companies to appoint independent directors to serve on key committees, such as the **audit committee** and **risk management committee**. These directors are responsible for ensuring that the financial statements present an accurate reflection of the company's performance and that internal controls are robust enough to prevent **fraudulent activities** like insider trading.

How Forward-Looking Statements in MD&A (Management Discussion and Analysis) Impact Stock Prices

The **Management Discussion and Analysis (MD&A)** section of an annual report is where company executives provide a narrative on the company's financial performance, risk factors, and strategic outlook. While financial statements present historical data, the MD&A contains **forward-looking statements** that outline future expectations, goals, and uncertainties.

1. Impact of Forward-Looking Statements on Stock Prices

Forward-looking statements in the MD&A are closely scrutinized by investors and analysts, as they offer insights into the company's future growth prospects and risk exposure. These statements often include forecasts on revenue growth, market expansion, R&D initiatives, and competitive positioning. When a company's **future guidance** is optimistic, it can lead to a surge in stock prices, as investors anticipate strong future performance. Conversely, conservative guidance can cause a selloff as investors adjust their expectations downward.

- **Revenue and Profit Forecasts**: Positive revenue and profit forecasts often lead to **buying pressure**, especially from institutional investors, as they reassess the company's valuation. For example, if a technology company projects double-digit revenue growth in emerging markets due to new product launches, its stock price may experience a significant uptick.

- **Risk Disclosures**: Forward-looking statements also contain **risk disclosures**, highlighting potential headwinds such as regulatory challenges, currency fluctuations, or rising input costs. These risks provide valuable information for investors in determining whether to adjust their exposure to the company. A company that discloses risks about its supply chain or litigation could experience a drop in stock price as investors price in potential downside risks.

2. Legal Implications of Forward-Looking Statements

While forward-looking statements are critical for investor decision-making, they must comply with regulatory guidelines to avoid misleading the market. In the U.S., forward-looking statements are governed by the **Private Securities Litigation Reform Act of 1995 (PSLRA)**, which provides a safe harbour for companies making projections as long as they are accompanied by meaningful cautionary statements about risks. **In India,** SEBI's regulations require that forward-looking statements be grounded in realistic assumptions and disclosed in a way that does not mislead investors.

Companies that fail to provide accurate or reasonable forward-looking statements can face **securities class action lawsuits** if shareholders believe they were misled by overly optimistic or false projections. These legal actions can severely damage a company's reputation and lead to substantial financial penalties.

Conclusion

Corporate transparency and financial disclosure are fundamental to maintaining **market integrity**, building investor trust, and preventing fraudulent activities like insider trading. Through comprehensive annual reports, robust corporate governance, diligent audits, and detailed forward-looking statements, companies provide the vital information that market participants need to make informed decisions. However, the misuse or misrepresentation of these disclosures can lead to significant financial consequences and undermine investor confidence.

Ensuring transparency is not just a regulatory requirement but a critical component of sustaining long-term value creation for shareholders and protecting the integrity of global financial markets. As regulatory frameworks continue to evolve and market complexities grow, companies must remain vigilant in their disclosure practices to avoid legal pitfalls and safeguard their reputations.

Chapter 5

The Anatomy of Insider Trading Policies

In an era of heightened corporate scrutiny, **insider trading policies** are no longer optional safeguards—they are **"essential components"** of a company's governance framework. As global markets become more integrated and the stakes for regulatory non-compliance rise, having a well-crafted, dynamic insider trading policy is critical for ensuring transparency, protecting corporate integrity, and safeguarding both employees and the firm from legal and reputational risks. This chapter explores the anatomy of insider trading policies, delving into the key mechanisms and global best practices that enable corporations to effectively mitigate insider trading risks.

The Core Elements of a Corporate Insider Trading Policy

The foundation of any insider trading policy lies in its ability to enforce **clear boundaries** for employees and executives who have access to **Material Non-Public Information (MNPI)**. These policies must not only comply with legal regulations but also foster an ethical culture of transparency and integrity.

1. Defining Insiders: Who is Covered?

A comprehensive policy begins by explicitly defining who qualifies as an **insider**. While senior executives and board members are automatically included, companies must go beyond the obvious by covering any individual with access to MNPI. This includes:

- **C-suite executives and directors;**
- **Employees across finance, legal, and strategy divisions;**
- **External consultants, auditors, and even legal advisors;** who may come into contact with sensitive data.

By broadening the scope, companies ensure that all key players are aware of their legal obligations, leaving no room for ambiguity.

2. MNPI: Clarifying What is Material Information

Insiders must fully understand what constitutes MNPI, which includes any non-public information that could affect the company's stock price. MNPI might include:

- **Earnings reports**: Unreleased financial data or profit warnings
- **Mergers, acquisitions, or divestitures**: Any strategic corporate actions that may affect valuation
- **Product launches**: Market-moving innovations or failures
- **Litigation**: Lawsuits or regulatory actions that could impact financial performance

This element of the policy needs to be communicated with precision, often through regular training and real-time monitoring to ensure full compliance.

3. Trading Windows and Blackout Periods: Structuring Safe Zones

Blackout periods prevent insiders from trading during critical times when MNPI is being finalized but not yet disclosed. In contrast, **trading windows** are periods when insiders can trade safely, typically after earnings announcements or significant news has been made public.

- **Earnings blackout periods**: Often start 15-30 days before quarterly or annual earnings releases and end 24-48 hours after the earnings call.
- **Strategic blackout periods**: Occur during major corporate events such as mergers, acquisitions, or legal proceedings. These blackouts ensure that insiders do not exploit pre-disclosed information.

Creating and communicating clear trading windows and blackout periods reduces the risk of insider trading and instils investor confidence that executives are not using privileged information for personal gain.

4. Pre-Clearance Requirements: An Extra Layer of Oversight

In many corporations, insiders are required to **pre-clear** any proposed trade before execution. This ensures that compliance teams can review the request and determine if the trade aligns with internal policies and regulations.

- **AI-Powered Compliance Tools**: Increasingly, companies are integrating **AI-driven Systems** to automate the pre-clearance process. These systems instantly flag any conflicts of interest, review an individual's historical trades, and monitor market conditions to ensure that no violation of MNPI occurs.

5. Disclosure Obligations and Reporting

Transparency is key in any insider trading policy. Most companies require insiders to disclose their stock holdings periodically, as well as any changes to these holdings. In the U.S., for example, insiders must file "**Form 4**" with the SEC within two business days of any trade.

- **Internal Disclosures**: Some companies also mandate internal reporting, providing an additional safeguard by ensuring that the compliance team is aware of all trades before they happen.

6. Sanctions and Consequences

A robust insider trading policy clearly defines the sanctions for any violations, ranging from internal disciplinary actions to legal consequences. These must be severe enough to act as a deterrent, with clear alignment to local and international regulations such as **SEBI's Prohibition of Insider Trading Regulations (2015)** in India or **SEC Rule 10b-5** in the U.S.

High-profile insider trading cases often result in significant fines, reputational damage, and imprisonment, underscoring the importance of adherence to a strict policy.

Pre-Clearance Requirements, Blackout Periods, and Trading Windows

The interplay between **pre-clearance**, **blackout periods**, and **trading windows** forms the backbone of most insider trading policies, providing a structured and compliant framework for insiders to execute trades without the risk of inadvertently violating securities laws.

Pre-Clearance Procedures: Precision and Real-Time Monitoring

Pre-clearance is a critical element that protects both the company and the individual from unintentional violations. For example:

- **Compliance-First Approach**: Insiders submit a trade request to the compliance department or legal counsel before executing any transaction. This enables the compliance team to review the insider's trading history, current market dynamics, and any pending MNPI that could potentially make the trade illegal.

- **Automated Clearance Systems**: As firms increasingly turn to **automation**, pre-clearance systems leverage **big data analytics** to scan for possible conflicts, flagging trades that may overlap with blackout periods or coincide with significant corporate events.

Blackout Periods: Ensuring Compliance in Sensitive Times

Blackout periods are the cornerstone of insider trading policies, ensuring that insiders are prohibited from trading during sensitive periods when MNPI is being developed but has not yet been publicly disclosed.

For example, a **technology company** like **Apple** might impose blackout periods around its product launches, where the stakes for insider trading violations are particularly high due to the potential market-moving nature of such events.

Blackout periods are designed to level the playing field and prevent any exploitation of privileged information. By clearly defining these periods and communicating them well in advance, companies can minimize the risk of insider trading violations.

Trading Windows: Safe Zones for Insiders

Trading windows open after the release of significant corporate news, ensuring that insiders have the same level of public information as general investors. These windows typically last for a limited time, such as 5-10 days after quarterly earnings are released, allowing insiders to execute trades within a compliant framework.

Building a Culture of Compliance: Internal Monitoring and Auditing Systems

A company's insider trading policy is only as strong as its **compliance culture**. By developing a proactive compliance framework, companies can better prevent violations, promote ethical behaviour, and maintain investor confidence.

1. Advanced Monitoring Systems

Advanced monitoring systems enable companies to detect and prevent suspicious activity. Modern **surveillance systems**, powered by **machine learning algorithms**, are capable of:

- **Real-Time Monitoring**: These systems continuously scan for unusual trading patterns, such as large, coordinated trades or spikes in activity near critical blackout periods.

- **Anomaly Detection**: By using **historical trade data** and comparing it against current trades, machine learning systems can flag trades that deviate from normal patterns, allowing compliance teams to investigate potential insider trading before it occurs.

Case Study: **JP Morgan** uses an AI-driven system to analyze millions of trades per day, enabling compliance teams to flag any anomalies and take preventive action. These systems analyze both "**trading behaviour and insider access to MNPI**", ensuring that even the most sophisticated attempts at insider trading are caught before they become serious violations.

2. Routine Compliance Audits

Routine compliance audits are a crucial part of maintaining transparency. These audits evaluate whether employees are adhering to insider trading rules and examine if the policy itself is robust enough to handle evolving market conditions.

- **Internal Audits**: Regular internal audits help ensure that any internal control failures are identified early, while compliance departments conduct thorough reviews of insider trading requests and trading histories.

- **External Audits**: Engaging external auditors brings an additional layer of objectivity, ensuring that the company is fully aligned with regulatory requirements.

3. Employee Training and Awareness Programs

Establishing a strong **compliance culture** starts with education. Employees—especially those with regular access to MNPI—should undergo **regular training programs** focused on the importance of adhering to insider trading policies. This training typically includes:

- **Scenario-Based Learning**: Using real-world case studies to show how inadvertent violations can occur.
- **Best Practices**: Training employees on how to handle MNPI and avoid accidental disclosures.

Companies like **Microsoft** have developed sophisticated training modules for executives and high-risk employees, ensuring they fully understand how and when they can trade company securities.

Global Best Practices in Insider Trading Policies: Case Studies from Top Firms

The most effective insider trading policies combine regulatory compliance with a strong internal governance framework. Leading global companies have taken these principles to the next level by integrating advanced technologies and rigorous oversight.

Case Study 1: Goldman Sachs

Goldman Sachs' insider trading policy is widely regarded as one of the most stringent in the financial sector. The firm enforces a **multi-tiered pre-clearance process**, where all insider trading requests are routed through both legal and compliance teams for approval.

- **Automated Pre-Clearance**: Goldman's automated system immediately flags high-risk trades, reducing the chance of human error and ensuring full compliance with SEC rules.
- **Post-Trade Audits**: After trades are completed, they are subject to a post-trade audit to ensure there were no last-minute violations of MNPI rules.

Case Study 2: Tesla

Tesla implements an aggressive policy on **blackout periods** and trading windows. The company mandates extended blackout periods for executives and key employees, especially around product announcements and earnings calls.

- **Extended Blackout Periods**: Tesla enforces 45-day blackout periods before earnings and major announcements to minimize any risk of insider trading. This ensures that any sensitive information related to their cutting-edge technology developments is tightly controlled.

Case Study 3: HSBC

As one of the world's largest multinational banks, HSBC integrates global regulatory requirements with local policies to create a comprehensive insider trading compliance framework.

- **Geo-Targeted Compliance**: HSBC's **geo-targeted compliance systems** prevent employees from trading in markets where they possess MNPI, ensuring that local and international regulatory requirements are adhered to without conflict.

Conclusion

The anatomy of insider trading policies must be meticulously crafted to address both legal requirements and ethical considerations. By focusing on **pre-clearance procedures, blackout periods, trading windows,** and a strong culture of compliance, companies can protect themselves from the legal and reputational risks of insider trading. Through **advanced AI-driven monitoring systems** and regular audits, firms can stay ahead of evolving risks, ensuring that their policies remain not only compliant but exemplary in global best practices.

Case studies from top global firms like **Goldman Sachs**, **Tesla**, and **HSBC** underscore the importance of innovation and rigor in crafting these policies. As the regulatory landscape continues to evolve, so too must insider trading policies, ensuring they remain resilient, dynamic, and aligned with global standards.

Chapter 6

How SEBI Detects Insider Trading

The **Securities and Exchange Board of India (SEBI)** employs advanced technologies and surveillance systems to combat insider trading, a significant threat to the integrity of financial markets. As financial markets become increasingly global and complex, SEBI has integrated cutting-edge tools to detect insider trading with a focus on real-time monitoring, algorithmic trading, and forensic analysis. In this chapter, we explore SEBI's sophisticated techniques, compare them with international regulatory practices, and examine notable insider trading cases from India and abroad.

Advanced Surveillance Tools: IMSS (Integrated Market Surveillance System) and TAS (Trade Analytics Software)

SEBI has developed an extensive toolkit to monitor market activity and detect suspicious trading patterns. Two of its most important tools are the **Integrated Market Surveillance System (IMSS)** and **Trade Analytics Software (TAS)**. These systems provide SEBI with real-time data and post-trade forensic capabilities, allowing it to detect and investigate insider trading.

1. Integrated Market Surveillance System (IMSS)

The **IMSS** is SEBI's primary surveillance engine, capable of analysing vast amounts of market data in real-time. IMSS aggregates data from multiple trading platforms, including the **National Stock Exchange (NSE), Bombay Stock Exchange (BSE)**, and other major exchanges. The system is designed to capture and analyse every trade in India's capital markets, allowing SEBI to spot irregularities that may indicate insider trading or other market abuses.

- **High-Frequency Monitoring**: The IMSS is designed to capture trades executed in milliseconds, a critical capability for detecting **high-frequency trading (HFT)** strategies that might be used to mask insider trading. By analysing data points such as order timing, size, and price movements, IMSS can detect unusual trading patterns that suggest manipulation.

- **Price and Volume Anomalies**: IMSS uses sophisticated **machine learning algorithms** to detect price and volume anomalies. For instance, a sharp rise in trading volume just before an earnings announcement or a stock price moving sharply without any public information can trigger an alert within the system, flagging it for further investigation by SEBI.

2. Trade Analytics Software (TAS)

TAS is a post-trade analytical tool that SEBI uses for forensic analysis of trading activities. This software allows SEBI to drill down into individual trades and identify patterns that may be indicative of insider trading. TAS has been crucial in SEBI's ability to analyze massive data sets, track relationships between different market participants, and understand the dynamics of suspicious trading activity.

- **Volume Spike Detection**: TAS excels at identifying sudden spikes in trade volume or abnormal trading behaviour around material events such as earnings releases, mergers, or regulatory announcements. TAS compares current trading activity with historical data to highlight deviations that warrant investigation.

- **Algorithmic Trade Analysis**: TAS also monitors **algorithmic trading** strategies, where traders might attempt to disguise their actions by breaking large trades into smaller, algorithm-driven trades across multiple accounts or brokers. By using **pattern recognition algorithms**, TAS can link seemingly unconnected trades and uncover insider networks.

3. Latest Software Tools in Use

In addition to IMSS and TAS, SEBI and other global exchanges use cutting-edge software platforms to monitor and analyse market activity:

- **SMARTS** (Market Surveillance by **NASDAQ**): SMARTS is a powerful global surveillance platform used by exchanges and regulators worldwide, including SEBI. It uses **real-time analytics** to monitor trading behaviour, identify potential market abuse, and detect insider trading by analysing cross-market activity. SMARTS can identify complex manipulation schemes, such as **quote stuffing** and **layering**, which are techniques used in high-frequency trading.

- **ACTS (Advanced Analytical Trading Surveillance)**: Deployed by global exchanges like **Euronext** and **Deutsche Börse**, ACTS uses **big data analytics** and **behavioural pattern recognition** to spot insider trading. It integrates with data from multiple markets to detect **cross-border manipulations**.

- **SCORES (SEBI Complaints Redress System)**: Although primarily used for handling investor complaints, **SCORES** also provides a database of previous market violations, helping SEBI cross-reference ongoing investigations with historical insider trading cases to identify patterns and potential repeat offenders.

International Systems for Surveillance

SEBI's surveillance approach is in line with international practices, and major exchanges around the world use similar advanced tools:

- **MIDAS (Market Information Data Analytics System) – U.S. SEC:** The **SEC** uses **MIDAS**, which captures millions of trades and quotes every day, providing the SEC with an in-depth understanding of market activities. MIDAS helps the SEC identify suspicious trading behaviour by analysing time-series data, including the impact of **order book depth** and **execution speeds** on stock prices.

- **Zenith – FCA (U.K.):** The **Financial Conduct Authority (FCA)** in the U.K. relies on the **Zenith Market Surveillance System**, which uses **artificial intelligence** to track suspicious trades across global markets. Zenith is particularly adept at analysing trades made through **dark pools**, private exchanges where large transactions are made with limited visibility to the public.

Detecting Insider Trading: Market Pattern Analysis, Algorithmic Trading Anomalies, and Volume Spikes

Detecting insider trading requires advanced analytical tools capable of processing and interpreting vast amounts of financial data in real-time. SEBI and other regulators use techniques like **market pattern analysis, algorithmic trading anomaly detection**, and **volume spike analysis** to spot trades that deviate from normal market behaviour.

1. Market Pattern Analysis

SEBI's IMSS and TAS systems are designed to track market activity around sensitive corporate events such as mergers, earnings releases, and regulatory changes. Market pattern analysis involves examining the **correlation** between price movements, trade volumes, and the timing of trades.

- **Pre-Announcement Spikes**: An insider trader might act on MNPI (Material Non-Public Information) by purchasing large volumes of a stock before a positive earnings release or selling off shares before negative news. SEBI's systems detect these **volume spikes** and **price swings** that occur without any public catalyst.

2. Algorithmic Trading Anomalies

Insider traders increasingly use algorithmic trading to evade detection by breaking large trades into smaller transactions, distributed over time or across multiple accounts.

SEBI's systems analyse high-frequency data to detect anomalies in **order execution, latency arbitrage**, and **quote stuffing**.

- **Latency Arbitrage**: SEBI focuses on traders who exploit differences in the speed at which information is disseminated across exchanges. Traders with **ultra-low latency** access to markets may execute trades milliseconds ahead of the general market based on non-public information. Systems like **SMARTS** and **MIDAS** flag these strategies by analysing **sub-millisecond execution times** and patterns in trade bursts.

- **Quote Stuffing and Layering**: Techniques like **quote stuffing** (placing and cancelling large numbers of orders to create a false impression of market demand) are commonly used in **High-Frequency Trading (HFT)** to manipulate markets. SEBI's tools detect such patterns by monitoring **order-to-trade ratios** and abnormal **cancellation rates**.

3. Volume Spikes and Suspicious Timing

Volume spikes around corporate announcements are a key indicator of potential insider trading. SEBI uses both IMSS and TAS to detect unusual volume surges that deviate from historical trading patterns.

- **Case Example: RIL (Reliance Industries Limited)**: In 2007, SEBI detected abnormal trading volume in **Reliance Industries** just days before the company's announcement of a major restructuring. SEBI used its volume spike detection tools in TAS to identify coordinated trades across multiple accounts linked to insiders. This led to significant fines and sanctions for market manipulation.

International Example: U.S. SEC vs. Raj Rajaratnam (Galleon Group)

The **SEC** utilized market surveillance tools like **MIDAS** to track **Raj Rajaratnam**'s trades before key corporate announcements. Rajaratnam orchestrated a complex network of corporate insiders at companies like **Intel** and **Goldman Sachs** to obtain MNPI and execute profitable trades ahead of earnings announcements. The SEC's investigation, which focused on trading volume spikes and abnormal price movements, resulted in one of the largest insider trading convictions in U.S. history.

The Legal and Practical Challenges SEBI Faces in Enforcement

Despite SEBI's advanced technologies, it faces several legal and practical challenges in prosecuting insider trading cases. The **burden of proof** remains a significant obstacle, as SEBI must not only show that an insider had access to MNPI but also prove intent.

1. Proving Intent

Insider trading cases are challenging to prosecute because they often rely on circumstantial evidence. While SEBI's systems can detect suspicious trades, proving that a trader knowingly acted on MNPI is difficult.

- **Communications Evidence**: SEBI increasingly relies on communications evidence such as emails, phone logs, and social media interactions to establish intent.

However, obtaining this evidence requires navigating **data privacy laws**, and traders may use encrypted messaging platforms to evade detection.

2. Cross-Border Trading and Jurisdictional Issues

Cross-border trading poses a significant challenge to SEBI's enforcement efforts. Traders may execute insider trades on foreign exchanges, complicating SEBI's ability to investigate.

- **Memoranda of Understanding (MoUs)**: SEBI has signed MoUs with international regulators such as the **SEC** (U.S.) and **FCA** (U.K.) to facilitate the exchange of information. However, differences in legal frameworks and data-sharing agreements can slow down investigations.

3. Data Privacy and Compliance

SEBI must also comply with **data privacy regulations** such as the **Information Technology Act**. Gaining access to traders' personal communications or financial records requires court approvals, which can delay investigations.

Real-World Investigations: How SEBI's Forensic Approach Has Evolved

SEBI's approach to insider trading has evolved significantly, particularly with the integration of forensic data analysis. This shift allows SEBI to conduct more thorough investigations, tracking the flow of MNPI and linking trades across multiple accounts.

1. **Forensic Data Analysis**

SEBI employs forensic accounting techniques to analyze traders' financial transactions and identify links between market participants. This approach was instrumental in major cases such as:

- **SEBI vs. Bhavesh Shah (Gujarat NRE Coke Ltd.)**: In this case, SEBI used forensic data analysis to trace trades linked to Shah's insider knowledge of a corporate restructuring plan. By tracking account linkages and financial flows, SEBI secured significant penalties and a lifetime trading ban for Shah.

2. **Technological Evolution of SEBI's Enforcement**

SEBI's adoption of **AI-driven tools** and **big data analytics** has enhanced its ability to detect insider trading in real-time. The integration of **predictive analytics** enables SEBI to forecast potential insider trading risks by identifying early warning signals in market data.

Conclusion

SEBI's detection of insider trading relies on cutting-edge technologies such as **IMSS** and **TAS**, complemented by global surveillance tools like **SMARTS** and **MIDAS**. The integration of AI-driven analytics and forensic approaches has significantly enhanced SEBI's ability to detect and prosecute insider trading, although challenges such as proving intent, navigating cross-border trades, and adhering to data privacy laws remain. By continuing to evolve its surveillance capabilities and collaborating with international regulators, SEBI is positioned to maintain the integrity of India's financial markets.

Chapter 7

International Regulatory Frameworks for Insider Trading

In today's interconnected financial world, insider trading knows no borders, making it essential for regulatory bodies worldwide to adopt strong frameworks and foster international cooperation to safeguard market integrity. Authorities such as the **Securities and Exchange Commission (SEC)** in the United States, the **Financial Conduct Authority (FCA)** in the United Kingdom, and SEBI in India have developed comprehensive regulations to combat insider trading. However, enforcing these laws on a global scale, especially in emerging markets, presents unique challenges that demand advanced surveillance tools and collaborative international strategies. This delves into the core aspects of **international insider trading regulations**, highlighting how these rules influence market behaviour and drive enforcement actions across jurisdictions.

The SEC's Rule 10b-5 and Its Impact on Global Insider Trading Enforcement

The **U.S. Securities and Exchange Commission (SEC)** has long been regarded as a global leader in securities regulation, and its **Rule 10b-5**, established under the **Securities Exchange Act of 1934**, remains one of the most powerful tools in combating insider trading globally. This rule prohibits any act or omission resulting in fraud or deceit in connection with the purchase or sale of any security, making it the cornerstone of the SEC's insider trading enforcement.

1. Rule 10b-5: The Global Gold Standard for Insider Trading Regulation

Rule 10b-5 prohibits trading on **Material Non-Public Information (MNPI)** and extends to both primary violators (those directly involved in the insider trading) and secondary actors (those who aid and abet the conduct). The rule's broad applicability has set a precedent for how insider trading is regulated worldwide, influencing regulatory bodies across jurisdictions.

- **Material Information**: The SEC defines material information as any data that would significantly affect an investor's decision-making process. This includes earnings reports, mergers, acquisitions, and strategic developments. By using an expansive interpretation of what constitutes **materiality**, **Rule 10b-5** has made it easier for regulators to prosecute insider trading violations.

- **International Impact**: The SEC's approach to insider trading enforcement, particularly under **Rule 10b-5**, has had a far-reaching influence. Regulatory bodies in **Canada**, **Australia**, and **Hong Kong** have incorporated aspects of the **SEC's** enforcement model into their own frameworks, making **Rule 10b-5** a **de-facto** global standard for insider trading regulation.

2. High-Profile SEC Cases and Their Global Ramifications

The SEC's insider trading cases often serve as global benchmarks for enforcement strategies. For instance, the **Raj Rajaratnam** case, in which the founder of **Galleon Group** was convicted of insider trading, not only set a precedent in the U.S. but also encouraged regulatory bodies across Europe and Asia to tighten their surveillance and enforcement mechanisms.

- **Use of Wiretaps**: The SEC's groundbreaking use of wiretaps in this case, a method typically reserved for criminal investigations, demonstrated the lengths to which regulators could go to gather evidence against insider trading. This case has been referenced by international regulators, such as the **Australian Securities and Investments Commission (ASIC)**, in their own high-profile investigations.

FCA's Market Abuse Regulation (MAR): A Comprehensive Look at Europe's Legal Framework

Europe has a highly sophisticated and rigorous approach to market abuse, particularly insider trading, which is primarily governed by the **Market Abuse Regulation (MAR)**. Enforced by the **Financial Conduct Authority (FCA)** in the U.K. and other European Union regulators, MAR provides a **pan-European framework** that standardizes the rules around insider trading and market manipulation.

1. Market Abuse Regulation (MAR): The Foundation of European Insider Trading Law

MAR came into force in 2016, replacing the **Market Abuse Directive (MAD)**, and applies to all securities traded on regulated markets, **Multilateral Trading Facilities (MTFs)**, and **Organized Trading Facilities (OTFs)**. MAR covers a broad range of **market abuse behaviours**, including insider trading, market manipulation, and unlawful disclosure of inside information.

- **Broad Scope of MAR**: MAR applies to a wide range of instruments, including stocks, bonds, derivatives, and emissions allowances, creating a holistic approach to combating insider trading across Europe's fragmented financial markets. It also introduces stricter reporting obligations for market participants and enhanced **transparency requirements** for listed companies.

- **Insider Lists**: One of the key elements of MAR is the requirement for companies to maintain **insider lists**—detailed logs of all individuals who have access to MNPI. These lists must be updated in real time, providing regulators with the ability to track the flow of inside information.

2. FCA's Surveillance Tools and Enforcement Mechanisms

The FCA utilizes state-of-the-art surveillance systems like **Zenith** and **Siren** to detect suspicious trading patterns across U.K. markets. These systems enable the FCA to conduct **cross-market surveillance**, analyse trade execution data, and flag potential insider trading based on deviations from established market norms.

- **Zenith System**: The **Zenith Surveillance System** is specifically designed to detect **algorithmic trading abuses** and **cross-border insider trading**. By analysing high-frequency trading patterns, Zenith flags trades that appear to be coordinated or designed to exploit latency differences between exchanges.

- **Algorithmic Market Abuse**: Given the increasing reliance on **high-frequency trading (HFT)**, the FCA's use of **pattern recognition software** allows regulators to identify and investigate insider traders using sophisticated algorithms to exploit market-moving information. The system's ability to track algorithmic activity across multiple exchanges provides a critical tool for tackling modern market abuse schemes.

3. Key FCA Case: FCA vs. Martyn Dodgson

In one of the largest insider trading cases in the U.K., **Martyn Dodgson**, a former Deutsche Bank director, was convicted under MAR for passing MNPI to associates who traded on the information. The FCA's use of **electronic surveillance** and **forensic accounting** helped uncover Dodgson's complex network of trades, leading to significant fines and lengthy prison sentences for those involved. This case underscored the FCA's commitment to using cutting-edge technology to detect and prosecute insider trading.

Cross-Border Cooperation: How SEBI Collaborates with International Regulatory Bodies

In the age of globalization, insider trading is often a cross-border crime, with perpetrators executing trades on foreign exchanges to evade local regulations. To tackle these challenges,

SEBI has established partnerships with international regulatory bodies, enabling **real-time data sharing**, coordinated investigations, and joint enforcement actions.

1. Memoranda of Understanding (MoUs) with Global Regulators

SEBI has signed several **Memoranda of Understanding (MoUs)** with key global regulatory bodies, including the **SEC, FCA**, and **European Securities and Markets Authority (ESMA)**, to enhance cross-border cooperation. These agreements facilitate the exchange of information related to suspicious trades, enable joint investigations, and streamline enforcement efforts across jurisdictions.

- **Cooperative Surveillance**: SEBI works closely with international regulators to identify insider trading schemes that span multiple markets. For example, if an Indian insider trader executes trades on a U.S. exchange, the SEC and SEBI collaborate to track the flow of information, trades, and profits across borders.

- **International Data Sharing**: SEBI's collaboration with the **International Organization of Securities Commissions (IOSCO)** allows for **real-time data exchanges** between regulators in different countries. This collaboration helps SEBI obtain crucial evidence for its investigations, such as foreign bank account records and trading histories.

2. Joint Investigations and Case Studies

SEBI has worked on multiple high-profile insider trading cases that required international cooperation. For example, in a case involving **Satyam Computer Services**, SEBI coordinated with the SEC to investigate suspicious trading activities linked to the company's financial misstatements. The joint investigation uncovered fraudulent trades executed by company insiders in both India and the U.S., leading to significant sanctions.

- **Foreign Example: SEC vs. Petrobras**: The SEC's insider trading investigation into **Petrobras**, a state-owned Brazilian oil company, is another example of cross-border regulatory collaboration. Petrobras was involved in a massive insider trading and bribery scandal that implicated executives, government officials, and traders in both Brazil and the U.S. By working closely with Brazilian regulators, the SEC was able to secure critical evidence, leading to hefty fines and settlements.

Insider Trading Regulations in Emerging Markets: Challenges and Solutions

Emerging markets often face unique challenges in enforcing insider trading laws, such as limited resources, outdated technologies, and fragmented regulatory frameworks. However, many emerging market regulators, including SEBI, have made significant strides in modernizing their enforcement mechanisms and collaborating with global regulators.

1. Key Challenges in Emerging Markets

- **Lack of Sophisticated Surveillance Tools**: Many emerging markets lack the advanced surveillance technologies used by regulators in developed markets, making it difficult to detect complex insider trading schemes. In markets like **Vietnam** and **Nigeria**, regulators often rely on manual reviews of trading activity, limiting their ability to identify **high-frequency trading abuses** or **cross-market manipulations**.

- **Weak Legal Frameworks**: Insider trading laws in some emerging markets are not as comprehensive or strictly enforced as in developed markets. This creates loopholes for traders to exploit MNPI without facing significant penalties. In countries like **Indonesia**, the lack of a unified legal framework for insider trading makes it challenging for regulators to pursue convictions.

2. SEBI's Role in Strengthening Emerging Market Regulations

As a leading regulator in one of the world's largest emerging markets, SEBI plays a crucial role in strengthening the enforcement of insider trading laws across the region. SEBI's adoption of advanced surveillance technologies, such as **IMSS** and **TAS**, has set a benchmark for other emerging market regulators. Through initiatives like **capacity-building programs** and **technical workshops**, SEBI has helped regulators in countries like **Sri Lanka**, **Bangladesh**, and **Nepal** enhance their insider trading detection capabilities.

- **Technology Transfers and Best Practices**: SEBI collaborates with international regulators to share best practices and technologies, enabling emerging markets to improve their insider trading detection frameworks. For example, SEBI has participated in technical assistance programs with **IOSCO**, helping other regulators implement **AI-driven trade surveillance systems**.

Conclusion

Insider trading regulations have evolved into a global framework, with regulatory bodies like the SEC, FCA, and SEBI leading the charge. The **SEC's Rule 10b-5** has set the global standard for insider trading enforcement, influencing how regulators around the world approach market abuse. Europe's **Market Abuse Regulation (MAR)**, enforced by the FCA, provides a comprehensive and sophisticated framework for detecting insider trading, while SEBI's cross-border cooperation efforts demonstrate the importance of international collaboration in tackling complex, multinational trading schemes.

Emerging markets, while facing unique challenges, are making significant strides in modernizing their enforcement mechanisms. Through the adoption of advanced technologies and collaboration with global regulators, these markets are closing the gap in insider trading regulation, ensuring that their financial systems remain transparent and fair for all participants.

Chapter 8

Trading Mechanisms and How They Can Be Manipulated

The global financial markets operate on complex trading mechanisms that, while designed to facilitate liquidity and efficiency, can also be exploited by insider traders. With the advent of advanced **fintech, high-frequency trading algorithms**, and **global liquidity pools**, these mechanisms offer opportunities for exploitation by those with **Material Non-Public Information (MNPI)**. This chapter explores how different trading strategies such as **intraday trading, high-frequency trading (HFT), limit orders**, and **market makers** can be used in market manipulation, leveraging cutting-edge international technologies and data-driven insights to examine how regulators are responding to these challenges.

1. Intraday Trading and High-Frequency Trading (HFT)

Intraday Trading: The Intersection of Speed and Strategy

Intraday trading involves buying and selling securities within the same trading session, capitalizing on short-term price movements. Insiders, especially those with privileged access to

MNPI, use intraday volatility to disguise their trades. By spreading trades throughout the day and taking advantage of minor price fluctuations, insiders can blend into the market without drawing suspicion.

- **Short-term Arbitrage**: Insiders may engage in **arbitrage** between stock prices on different exchanges by executing intraday trades that capture pricing inefficiencies. For example, a trader with MNPI might simultaneously buy shares on the **London Stock Exchange (LSE)** and sell them on the **New York Stock Exchange (NYSE)** when the same stock is trading at different prices across these platforms. This form of cross-market arbitrage leverages information asymmetry and the speed of execution that intraday trading offers.

- **Flash Crashes and Volatility Exploitation**: Insiders can exploit market volatility through **flash crashes**, which are sudden, sharp drops in stock prices triggered by high-speed trading algorithms. In these situations, insiders can place aggressive buy orders during the crash and sell once prices recover, taking advantage of the temporary mispricing created by algorithmic reactions. One of the most notable examples was the **2010 Flash Crash**, where the Dow Jones Industrial Average plunged nearly **1,000 points** in a matter of minutes before recovering.

High-Frequency Trading (HFT): Speed as a Market Weapon

High-frequency trading (HFT) has transformed global markets by allowing traders to execute thousands of transactions in milliseconds. For insiders with access to MNPI, HFT provides an ideal vehicle to profit from **market-moving information** before it becomes widely available. By using advanced algorithms and **co-located servers** (servers placed physically close to the exchange's servers to reduce latency), insider traders can outpace ordinary investors, executing trades based on MNPI milliseconds before the information impacts the broader market.

- **Algorithmic Execution**: Insiders may program algorithms to trade on **momentum strategies**, where the algorithm continuously buys or sells securities based on the price trends. When insiders are aware of forthcoming market-moving events, such as mergers or earnings releases, they adjust their algorithms to capitalize on the market reaction, entering and exiting positions at light speed.

- **Latency Arbitrage**: One of the most prominent HFT strategies is **latency arbitrage**, where traders exploit slight delays in the dissemination of price information between exchanges. Insiders with MNPI can act on this information across different exchanges, executing buy or sell orders on one exchange while the price is still adjusting on another. Latency arbitrage allows insiders to lock in risk-free profits by capitalizing on **information gaps** between exchanges.

International Example: Use of HFT in the SEC vs. DRW Trading Case

In the **SEC vs. DRW Trading Group** case, the **Securities and Exchange Commission (SEC)** accused DRW of using HFT strategies to manipulate **futures contracts**. DRW allegedly placed trades that influenced the settlement price of contracts by leveraging **electronic trading systems** and the speed advantage HFT offers. The firm was accused of exploiting latency differences and liquidity gaps, a common technique that insider traders can use to conceal their MNPI-driven trades.

Global Technologies in High-Frequency Trading

- **Xetra** (used by **Deutsche Börse**): **Xetra**, one of the most advanced electronic trading systems globally, enables high-frequency trading across European exchanges. By integrating with co-located servers, Xetra reduces execution times, providing high-frequency traders (HFTs) with a significant advantage in executing orders faster than the broader market.

- **FIX Protocol**: The **Financial Information eXchange (FIX)** protocol is a global messaging standard used to communicate pre-trade, trade, and post-trade data. HFT firms use FIX protocol messages to place orders at rapid speeds, allowing insiders with MNPI to issue multiple orders almost instantaneously.

2. Day Trading and Limit Orders in Insider Trading Context

Day Trading: Speed and Anonymity in Insider Transactions

Day trading, with its focus on short-term profits and rapid execution, provides insiders a way to execute large trades without alerting the market. Insiders, leveraging MNPI, can place **market orders** to capitalize on imminent corporate news, using the volatility generated by the announcement to their advantage.

- **Pattern Day Trading**: Many regulatory bodies, including the **SEC** and **FCA**, impose specific rules around **pattern day trading** to minimize market manipulation. Insiders, however, can sidestep these regulations by distributing trades across multiple brokerage accounts, avoiding the regulatory thresholds that would otherwise trigger compliance scrutiny.

- **Spoofing and Layering**: **Spoofing** involves placing large orders to buy or sell a stock without the intent to execute, creating a false impression of market demand or supply. Insiders can engage in spoofing to move the stock price in a direction favourable to their MNPI-driven strategy. Similarly, **layering** involves placing multiple limit orders at various price levels to manipulate the market perception of the stock's depth.

Global Regulations on Spoofing

International regulators, such as the **European Securities and Markets Authority (ESMA)** and the **Australian Securities and Investments Commission (ASIC),** have strengthened their rules against spoofing and layering. These manipulative practices are prohibited under the **Market Abuse Regulation (MAR)** in the European Union, which mandates strict reporting and order transparency requirements for institutional investors.

Limit Orders: A Mechanism for Masking Insider Activity

Limit orders allow insiders to control the execution price of their trades, helping them avoid detection by gradually buying or selling securities without causing significant price fluctuations. Limit orders are set to execute at a specific price or better, allowing insiders to place buy orders slightly below the market price or sell orders slightly above it. This ensures that insiders can still capitalize on MNPI while mitigating the risk of moving the market.

- **Dark Pools and Limit Orders**: Insiders often use **dark pools**, private exchanges where large trades are executed away from public scrutiny, in conjunction with limit orders. This enables them to trade large volumes of securities while minimizing the risk of triggering regulatory alarms. Dark pools are widely used across international exchanges, including **BATS Global Markets** and **Liquidnet**, providing insiders with anonymity.

- **VWAP Strategies**: Some insiders employ **Volume-Weighted Average Price (VWAP)** algorithms to further disguise their trading activity. VWAP-based strategies help ensure that insider trades are executed at the day's average price, reducing the likelihood of detection by market surveillance systems that monitor unusual trading volumes. VWAP strategies are particularly useful in **illiquid markets**, where small changes in order volume can have a significant impact on stock prices.

Case Study: Spoofing and Market Manipulation in the FCA vs. Michael Coscia

In a landmark case, **Michael Coscia**, a high-frequency trader, was convicted by the **FCA** and the **SEC** for engaging in spoofing to manipulate futures markets. Coscia used a layering strategy, placing multiple fake orders that were cancelled once the market reacted to them. This manipulation allowed him to profit from small price movements caused by his fake orders. The **case set a global precedent** for how regulators handle spoofing and market manipulation, showcasing the importance of sophisticated surveillance systems to detect such practices.

3. How Insiders Exploit Liquidity Gaps

Liquidity gaps present unique opportunities for insiders to exploit market inefficiencies. **Liquidity gaps** occur when there is a sudden lack of market participants willing to buy or sell a security, resulting in price gaps and volatility spikes. Insiders, armed with MNPI, can strategically place trades during these gaps to influence the stock's price trajectory without triggering suspicion.

Exploiting Low Liquidity Securities

Low-liquidity stocks, which typically have fewer active buyers and sellers, are particularly susceptible to price manipulation. Insiders may take advantage of this by executing trades during **off-peak trading hours**, where liquidity is thin. By accumulating or offloading shares in illiquid markets, insiders can artificially inflate or deflate stock prices, creating profitable opportunities that can be capitalized on once MNPI is disclosed.

- **Cross-Market Liquidity Arbitrage**: Insiders can use **cross-market liquidity arbitrage** to exploit differences in liquidity between international exchanges. For example, an insider might purchase shares in a U.S.-listed stock during low liquidity periods in Asian markets, where trading volumes are thinner. When liquidity returns during U.S. market hours, the insider can sell at a higher price, benefiting from the price gap created by their prior trade.

- **Impact of Low-Frequency Trading (LFT)**: While high-frequency trading focuses on speed, **low-frequency trading (LFT)** strategies are often employed by insiders in less liquid markets. Insiders can place **block trades**—large transactions executed through private negotiations—without immediately moving the stock price. These block trades are commonly executed in **emerging markets**, where liquidity is naturally lower and regulatory oversight may be less stringent.

Global Data on Liquidity Gaps

Studies by the **International Organization of Securities Commissions (IOSCO)** show that in emerging markets, such as **Brazil**, **India**, and **South Africa**, liquidity gaps tend to widen during periods of market stress, making these markets more susceptible to insider manipulation. The **bid-ask spread** in these markets increases by an average of **200-300%** during low liquidity periods, offering insiders greater opportunities to exploit price movements.

4. The Role of Market Makers in Insider Trading Investigations

Market makers are critical in ensuring liquidity and smooth trading in financial markets, but they also play a central role in investigations into insider trading. Market makers, who buy and sell securities to maintain liquidity, often have access to **order flow data** that can be used to front-run client trades or facilitate insider trading.

Order Flow and Front-Running Risks

Market makers have a unique vantage point in the market due to their access to real-time order flow data. This allows them to see large institutional trades before they are executed. In some cases, market makers might use this information to **front-run** large trades by placing their own orders ahead of the client's trade. When combined with MNPI, this practice enables market makers to profit from **non-public knowledge**.

- **Regulation and Oversight**: To prevent market makers from exploiting their role, regulators such as the **FCA**, **SEC**, and **SEBI** impose strict regulations on market makers, requiring them to report suspicious trading patterns and comply with **best execution** obligations. Market makers are also subject to routine audits, where regulators examine their trading activity for signs of market manipulation or insider trading.

Market Makers and Algorithmic Trading

In modern markets, many market makers use **algorithmic trading systems** to manage their order books. While these algorithms are designed to maintain market stability, they can also be manipulated by insiders working in collusion with market makers. For example, insiders might place large buy or sell orders that trigger the market maker's algorithm to adjust prices, creating profitable opportunities for the insider.

Example: Manipulation in the Libor Scandal

In the **Libor scandal**, major financial institutions, including **Barclays** and **UBS**, were accused of manipulating the **London Interbank Offered Rate (Libor)** with the help of market makers. While this case involved interest rate benchmarks rather than stock prices, it highlighted how market makers can collude with insiders to manipulate financial markets. The case led to a series of regulatory reforms, including stricter oversight of market makers and the introduction of more transparent pricing systems.

Conclusion

The trading mechanisms that underpin modern financial markets offer both opportunities for legitimate traders and risks of manipulation by those with access to MNPI. From the fast-paced world of **high-frequency trading (HFT)** to the deliberate exploitation of **liquidity gaps**, insiders use a variety of sophisticated strategies to profit from non-public information. Market makers, often seen as the gatekeepers of liquidity, also play a key role in both facilitating and investigating these activities.

Global regulators, including the **SEC**, **FCA**, and **SEBI**, continue to develop advanced **market surveillance systems** such as **SMARTS**, **Zenith**, and **ACTS**, employing **big data analytics**, **AI-driven algorithms**, and **cross-market monitoring** to detect and prevent insider trading. However, as technology evolves, so do the tactics of insider traders, making ongoing innovation in regulatory oversight and enforcement essential to maintaining **market integrity**.

Chapter 9

Aspects of Insider Trading and Economic Impact

Insider trading has long been a controversial practice in financial markets, impacting both **market efficiency** and **investor confidence**. The key question surrounding insider trading is whether it enhances market efficiency by bringing prices closer to their true value or whether it distorts price discovery, undermines trust, and creates unfair advantages. This chapter explores the **legal and illegal aspects of insider trading**, how **asymmetric information** leads to market manipulation, and the broader **economic consequences**, including price distortion, capital misallocation, and the erosion of investor confidence.

1. Legal vs. Illegal Insider Trading: Understanding the Fine Line

Insider trading is not always illegal; it is defined by the context and the **timing** of the trades. Distinguishing between **legal and illegal insider trading** is essential in understanding its implications for markets and the economy.

Legal Insider Trading: Transparency and Compliance

Legal insider trading occurs when corporate insiders—executives, directors, and other stakeholders—buy or sell stock in their own companies, provided they comply with the necessary **disclosure requirements**. In most jurisdictions, insiders are required to report their trades to regulatory bodies, such as **SEBI** in India, the **SEC** in the U.S., or the **FCA** in the U.K., using forms like the SEC's **Form 4**.

- **Scheduled Trades**: Some executives use **Rule 10b5-1 trading plans**, allowing them to schedule future trades according to pre-established criteria. This reduces the risk of being accused of trading on **material non-public information (MNPI)**, as these trades occur automatically, without the influence of insider knowledge.

- **Disclosure and Market Reaction**: When insiders legally buy or sell shares and report it to the market, their actions can influence **market sentiment**. For example, large insider purchases can signal confidence in the company's future, leading to price appreciation. Conversely, large sales may cause concern among investors about the company's prospects.

Illegal Insider Trading: Exploiting Asymmetric Information

Illegal insider trading involves buying or selling securities based on MNPI that is not available to the public. This practice undermines the principles of fairness and transparency, giving insiders an **unfair advantage** over regular investors. Illegal insider trading often involves **tipping**, where insiders share

MNPI with third parties, who then use that information to make trades.

- **Tippers and Tippees**: The **tipper** is the insider who shares MNPI, while the **tippee** is the person who receives and acts on it. Both the tipper and the tippee can be held liable for illegal insider trading, as seen in the **Raj Rajaratnam** case, where multiple layers of tippers and tippees were involved in a large insider trading network.

- **Penalties and Enforcement**: Regulatory bodies, such as SEBI, SEC, and FCA, impose strict penalties on those convicted of insider trading. These penalties include **fines, disgorgement of profits**, and **prison sentences**. In the **U.S.**, violators can face up to **20 years in prison** and fines of up to **$5 million** under the **Securities Exchange Act of 1934**.

Global Data on Insider Trading Convictions

According to a report by the **International Organization of Securities Commissions (IOSCO)**, insider trading convictions have increased by **35% globally** between 2015 and 2020, driven by improved surveillance tools and stricter enforcement. The report also noted that **cross-border investigations** now account for more than **40% of insider trading cases**, underscoring the global nature of the practice.

2. Asymmetric Information and Market Manipulation

The foundation of insider trading is **asymmetric information**—where insiders possess material information that is not available to the broader market. This imbalance creates opportunities for **market manipulation** and price distortion, which can have severe economic consequences.

Information Asymmetry: The Core of Insider Trading

Information asymmetry occurs when one party has access to information that another does not, leading to **inefficient market outcomes**. In the case of insider trading, corporate insiders, such as executives or board members, are privy to MNPI that can significantly impact stock prices. As a result, insiders can act on this information before the market has a chance to adjust, creating unfair advantages.

Types of Asymmetric Information:

- **Earnings Reports**: Insiders who know that the company is going to report higher-than-expected earnings can buy shares in advance, capitalizing on the subsequent price rise.

- **Mergers and Acquisitions**: Knowledge of pending mergers or acquisitions can lead to **merger arbitrage**, where insiders profit from the market's delayed response to acquisition news.

- **Product Launches or Failures**: Insiders with information about product launches, FDA approvals, or failures can buy or sell shares ahead of public announcements, distorting market behaviour.

Market Manipulation: Creating Inefficiencies through Information Gaps

Insiders use **information asymmetry** to manipulate the market, generating profits by taking advantage of the delayed market reaction to new information. This manipulation disrupts the **efficient market hypothesis (EMH)**, which suggests that all available information is reflected in asset prices.

- **Front-Running**: This occurs when insiders execute trades based on MNPI before the market becomes aware of it. For example, if an insider knows that a large institutional investor is about to place a significant buy order, they can buy shares ahead of the order and sell them at a higher price once the institutional order pushes the stock price up.

- **False Signals and Market Reactions**: Insider trading can create **false signals** for other market participants. If insiders sell large quantities of shares before bad news becomes public, it can create an **artificial drop in the stock price**, prompting other investors to sell, even though they do not know the real reason behind the price movement.

Case Study: Martha Stewart Insider Trading Scandal

In the **Martha Stewart** case, Stewart was convicted of insider trading for selling shares of **ImClone Systems** after receiving MNPI about the company's failed FDA approval. The sale occurred before the public knew of the decision, leading to significant losses for ordinary investors who were not aware of the MNPI. This case highlighted the economic damage that insider trading can cause, as it disrupted **price discovery** and **created distrust** in the fairness of the market.

3. Economic Consequences: Distorted Price Discovery and Capital Misallocation

Insider trading distorts the fundamental processes of **price discovery** and **capital allocation**, leading to **inefficiencies** in how financial markets operate. These inefficiencies can have long-lasting consequences for the broader economy, particularly in terms of investor behaviour, corporate governance, and market confidence.

Distorted Price Discovery: Undermining Market Efficiency

The purpose of financial markets is to enable **price discovery**, where asset prices reflect all available information. Insider trading disrupts this process by allowing a select few to act on MNPI, distorting the price signals that other market participants rely on. This mispricing can persist until the information becomes public, by which time insiders have already extracted their profits, leaving ordinary investors with **unrealized losses**.

- **Under-pricing and Overpricing**: Insiders buying shares based on positive MNPI can cause the stock to be **overpriced** once the news becomes public, as the initial run-up in the stock price reflects insider trades rather than genuine market demand. Conversely, insiders selling shares before bad news causes the stock to be **underpriced**, as the price does not reflect the true value of the information available to insiders.

- **Bid-Ask Spreads**: Research indicates that stocks affected by insider trading tend to have wider **bid-ask spreads**, as market makers adjust their prices to account for the higher risk of trading against insiders. This increases **transaction costs** for ordinary investors, further distorting price discovery.

Data on Price Distortion

A study by the **European Central Bank (ECB)** found that insider trading increases **market volatility** by **25%** and leads to a **3-5% mispricing** in stocks affected by significant insider trades. These distortions take longer to correct, especially in less liquid markets where price discovery is slower.

Capital Misallocation: Misguided Investment Decisions

Insider trading also leads to **capital misallocation**, where resources are diverted to inefficient uses due to inaccurate price signals. When market prices are artificially manipulated, investors allocate their capital based on faulty information, resulting in **suboptimal investment decisions**. This misallocation of resources can have broader economic consequences, as capital flows to less productive companies at the expense of more deserving firms.

- **Skewed Risk Perception**: Insider trading can give the impression that a company is performing better or worse than it truly is, leading to **misguided capital flows**. For instance, insiders might sell shares before negative news, causing other investors to prematurely sell as well, depriving the company of necessary capital for growth.

- **Reduced Long-Term Investment**: When investors perceive that markets are **rigged** or that insiders have an unfair advantage, they may be less willing to invest in **equity markets** for the long term. This reduction in market participation can decrease the overall pool of investment capital, leading to slower economic growth and innovation.

4. Effects on Investor Confidence and Market Participation

Insider trading erodes **investor confidence**, which is a cornerstone of healthy and efficient financial markets. When investors believe that markets are unfair or that insiders have an undue advantage, they are less likely to participate, leading to reduced liquidity and higher **costs of capital** for companies.

Erosion of Trust: The Investor Perspective

Trust is critical for the functioning of financial markets. Insider trading undermines this trust by creating a perception that markets are **manipulated** and that regular investors are at a disadvantage. This erosion of confidence can lead to a withdrawal from the market, reducing liquidity and increasing **volatility**.

- **Flight to Safety**: Investors may move their assets into **safer investments** like government bonds or real estate, where they perceive there is less risk of manipulation. This shift reduces the availability of capital for businesses looking to raise funds through equity markets.

- **Institutional Investor Hesitation**: Large institutional investors, such as pension funds and mutual funds, may hesitate to invest in companies or sectors where insider trading is prevalent. This hesitancy limits the ability of these institutions to allocate capital effectively, reducing their contribution to **economic growth**.

Market Participation and Liquidity Effects

Reduced investor confidence leads to **lower market participation**, which, in turn, affects **liquidity**. When liquidity decreases, it becomes more difficult for companies to raise funds, and the cost of capital increases. This, in turn, can slow down corporate growth and innovation, having a **negative impact on the broader economy**.

- **Liquidity Premium**: A lack of investor confidence often leads to a **liquidity premium**, where investors demand higher returns for holding stocks they perceive to be riskier due to insider trading. This increases the cost of equity for companies, making it more expensive to raise funds in public markets.

Global Insights on Investor Confidence

Data from the **World Bank** shows that emerging markets, where insider trading is more prevalent, have experienced a **25% decline in foreign portfolio investment** over the past decade. The lack of trust in market fairness has led to significant capital outflows, particularly in regions where regulatory enforcement is weak.

Conclusion

Insider trading has far-reaching consequences that extend beyond individual trades or corporate scandals. By exploiting **information asymmetry**, insider traders disrupt the fundamental processes of **price discovery**, **capital allocation**, and **investor trust**, which are essential for the functioning of healthy markets. The broader economic impact includes **distorted prices**, **misallocated capital**, and reduced market participation, all of which contribute to inefficiencies in the financial system.

As global regulators like **SEBI, SEC**, and **FCA** continue to develop more advanced tools to detect and prosecute insider trading, the challenge lies in balancing the need for **market transparency** with the complexity of modern financial markets. The economic cost of insider trading is not just borne by individual investors but by the economy at large, as capital flows are misdirected, and market confidence erodes.

Chapter 10

Prosecution and Legal Frameworks for Insider Trading

The legal prosecution of insider trading represents a multifaceted process involving advanced **forensic techniques**, global regulatory cooperation, and complex evidentiary standards. Both **SEBI** in India and the **Securities and Exchange Commission (SEC)** in the U.S., as well as other global regulators, have leveraged **forensic technologies** and **data analytics** to detect and prosecute insider trading. The use of forensic evidence—ranging from **communication logs** to **digital metadata**—has become essential in building strong cases, particularly in cases involving sophisticated networks of insiders and high-frequency traders. This chapter explores the forensic methodologies employed in insider trading prosecutions, focusing on **case studies**, the **legal frameworks** guiding these prosecutions, and the role of **civil vs. criminal proceedings**.

1. Prosecution Procedures for Insider Trading: SEBI and SEC Guidelines

Both SEBI and the SEC have adopted **forensic data analytics** as a critical component of their insider trading investigations, allowing them to detect patterns of illicit trading that would otherwise go unnoticed. Forensic evidence plays a key role in both **civil** and **criminal** proceedings, often serving as the backbone of successful prosecutions.

SEBI's Prosecution Framework: Leveraging Forensic Technologies

SEBI's **Prohibition of Insider Trading Regulations (2015)** establish strict guidelines for prosecuting insider trading, and forensic evidence is central to SEBI's investigative approach. As trading environments become increasingly digital, SEBI has deployed state-of-the-art technologies to trace **financial transactions**, **communication records**, and **market data** to uncover illegal trades.

Forensic Evidence in SEBI Investigations

- **Market Surveillance**: SEBI's **Integrated Market Surveillance System (IMSS)** and **Trade Analytics Software (TAS)** are designed to continuously monitor trading activity across multiple exchanges. Forensic tools within these systems use **pattern recognition algorithms** to flag unusual trades, such as **large-volume trades** just before earnings releases or **sudden price movements** ahead of mergers. These flags trigger deeper investigations where forensic teams analyse transaction-level data.

- **Digital Communication Forensics**: A significant component of SEBI's investigative process is tracking communication between insiders and external parties. By obtaining access to **emails**, **instant messaging platforms**, and **call logs**, SEBI can establish connections between suspected insiders and their tippees. In many cases, digital forensic experts are brought in to recover **deleted communications** or analyse **encrypted messages**, which often provide a direct link between MNPI and trading activity.

- **Example: SEBI vs. Gujarat NRE Coke Ltd.**: In this case, SEBI used forensic techniques to uncover the involvement of corporate insiders who had traded on MNPI regarding the company's restructuring. By analysing **phone records** and **email chains**, SEBI was able to prove that tip-offs were provided by key executives to a network of external traders. SEBI relied heavily on the recovered communications to build its case, leading to fines and trading bans for those involved.

Forensic Accounting Techniques

In addition to digital forensics, **forensic accounting** is a critical element in SEBI's prosecution of insider trading. SEBI uses forensic accountants to track the **flow of funds**, connect suspicious trades with specific accounts, and identify **irregular trading patterns**. By tracing the source of illicit profits, SEBI can establish a clear connection between insiders and their illegal trades, which is often used to support **disgorgement orders** and **asset freezes**.

- **Cross-Exchange Trading Analysis**: Forensic analysis in cross-exchange trading, where insiders may attempt to mask their activities by trading across multiple markets (e.g., NSE and BSE), involves the aggregation of trading data from different exchanges. SEBI's forensic experts analyse trading volumes, price fluctuations, and market depth to identify patterns suggesting that MNPI was used to inform these trades.

SEC's Prosecution Framework: Advanced Data and Forensic Tools

The SEC employs a combination of **forensic data analytics, surveillance technologies**, and **whistleblower-provided evidence** to build cases against insider traders. The SEC's forensic approach is geared toward tracking **high-frequency trades, cross-border transactions**, and **algorithmic trading anomalies**.

Key Forensic Tools and Techniques in SEC Investigations

- **MIDAS (Market Information Data Analytics System)**: **MIDAS** is the SEC's primary tool for analysing **trade execution data** across all U.S. exchanges. It aggregates billions of transactions, allowing forensic investigators to detect **microsecond-level trades** that may indicate insider trading or **market manipulation**. MIDAS is particularly effective at identifying **high-frequency trading (HFT)** strategies where insiders use **algorithms** to exploit MNPI.

  - **Algorithmic Trading Forensics**: The SEC has developed specific forensic techniques to analyse algorithmic trading patterns, especially in cases where insiders use **latency arbitrage** or **co-located servers** to trade milliseconds before the market reacts to news. By studying the trade execution timing and the algorithms' responses to **market-moving announcements**, forensic analysts can prove that MNPI was used to influence these trades.

- **CAT (Consolidated Audit Trail)**: The **Consolidated Audit Trail (CAT)** provides the SEC with an end-to-end view of all trading activities in U.S. markets, including the **time, price, and volume** of each trade. CAT helps forensic teams identify **suspicious trading clusters** by showing how orders were routed, filled, or cancelled. It also tracks **dark pool activity**, where insiders might execute trades outside of public exchanges to avoid scrutiny.

- **Forensic Email and Wiretap Evidence**: The SEC often relies on forensic analysis of **electronic communications**, including **emails, text messages, and wiretaps**. These digital records are used to show the intent behind trades and link insiders to external parties (tippees). In many high-profile cases, wiretaps have been instrumental in uncovering insider networks.

Case Study: SEC vs. Raj Rajaratnam – Wiretaps and Forensic Evidence

In the landmark **SEC vs. Raj Rajaratnam** case, forensic evidence played a pivotal role. The **SEC** and the **Department of Justice (DOJ)** used **wiretaps**, a tool traditionally associated with organized crime investigations, to record conversations between Rajaratnam and corporate insiders. These wiretaps provided direct evidence that Rajaratnam was receiving MNPI from executives at companies like **Goldman Sachs** and **Intel**, which he then used to execute highly profitable trades.

- **Digital Forensic Evidence**: The SEC also performed forensic analysis on Rajaratnam's **trading records**, linking the timing of his trades directly to the information he received through the wiretapped conversations. For example, Rajaratnam made trades in **Intel stock** just minutes after receiving inside information on the company's earnings. The combination of wiretaps, trade data, and financial forensics was critical in securing Rajaratnam's conviction, resulting in an **11-year prison sentence** and a **$92.8 million fine**.

2. Civil vs. Criminal Proceedings in Insider Trading Cases

In both civil and criminal proceedings, forensic evidence plays a critical role in establishing the connection between insiders and their illegal trades. The **standard of proof** differs between these two types of proceedings, but forensic evidence remains crucial in both.

Civil Proceedings: Financial Penalties and Disgorgement

In civil insider trading cases, regulators like SEBI and the SEC primarily seek **disgorgement of profits**, **fines**, and **trading bans**. The **burden of proof** in civil cases is lower than in criminal cases, relying on a **preponderance of the evidence** standard. This means that regulators must prove that it is more likely than not that insider trading occurred. Forensic evidence in civil proceedings often includes:

- **Trade Analytics and Timing Patterns**: Forensic data analysts examine the **timing of trades** relative to corporate announcements, comparing the behaviour of insiders with **market norms**. If the insider executed trades just before a **price-moving event** (e.g., a merger, earnings release, or product launch), forensic analysts highlight these patterns as evidence of MNPI-driven trading.

- **Digital Communication Logs**: Emails, texts, and other forms of communication are critical in civil cases, as they provide **context** for the timing and motivation behind trades. **For example**, if a CEO sent a confidential email to a friend about an upcoming acquisition, and the friend executed trades shortly after, these communications can serve as clear evidence of **tipping**.

Case Study: SEBI vs. Reliance Petroleum

In the **Reliance Petroleum** case, SEBI launched a civil investigation after detecting **abnormal trading volumes** just before a major announcement. Using forensic analysis, SEBI traced the trades back to key corporate insiders, demonstrating that they had leaked MNPI to outside brokers. SEBI imposed **substantial fines** and required the insiders to disgorge their illegal profits, further reinforcing the importance of forensic evidence in civil cases.

Criminal Proceedings: Severe Penalties and Imprisonment

Criminal prosecutions of insider trading are reserved for more egregious violations, where there is clear evidence of **wilful misconduct** and intent to deceive. The standard of proof in criminal cases is **beyond a reasonable doubt**, making forensic evidence particularly important in securing convictions.

- **Forensic Linkages Between Communication and Trading**: In criminal cases, forensic teams work to establish a direct link between **communications (emails, calls, or texts)** and the **trades themselves**. Prosecutors need to demonstrate that insiders knowingly used MNPI to make trades. This often involves reconstructing **deleted messages**, recovering **encrypted communications**, or even tracking **offshore accounts** used to store illicit gains.

- **Wiretaps and Surveillance**: In high-profile criminal cases like **SEC vs. Raj Rajaratnam**, wiretaps have been used to capture real-time conversations between insiders and their tippees. These recordings provide **irrefutable evidence** of the intent behind the trades. Additionally, **surveillance footage** and forensic analysis of financial transactions can further establish guilt by connecting the insiders' actions with market outcomes.

Case Study: U.K. FCA vs. Martyn Dodgson

The **Financial Conduct Authority (FCA)** in the U.K. successfully prosecuted **Martyn Dodgson**, a former Deutsche Bank director, using a combination of forensic analysis and communication records. Dodgson was part of a complex insider trading scheme that relied on tips about upcoming mergers and acquisitions. FCA forensic teams analysed **phone records**, **emails**, and **trading data**, linking Dodgson's communications with his trades. The court sentenced Dodgson to **5 years in prison** and ordered significant financial penalties.

3. Burden of Proof and Challenges in Prosecution

Proving insider trading requires overcoming significant challenges, especially when it comes to the **burden of proof**. Prosecutors must not only show that an individual had access to MNPI but also prove that the individual **knowingly** traded on that information.

Challenges in Proving Intent

Forensic evidence is often the key to proving intent, which is the most difficult element of insider trading cases. While regulators can easily track trading patterns, establishing that those trades were based on MNPI requires showing that the insider was aware of the information and that they acted deliberately to profit from it.

- **Circumstantial vs. Direct Evidence**: Forensic data can provide both circumstantial and direct evidence. Circumstantial evidence, such as **timing patterns** and **trading anomalies**, may suggest that the trader had access to MNPI. Direct evidence, such as **wiretaps**, **emails**, or **recorded meetings**, can provide conclusive proof that the insider acted on confidential information.

- **Cross-Border Challenges**: Insider trading often involves cross-border trades, complicating prosecution. Forensic experts must collaborate across jurisdictions to trace international trading flows, analyse offshore accounts, and recover communications that span different countries.

Example: Global Cooperation in the Petrobras Scandal

In the **Petrobras insider trading case**, regulators from multiple countries, including the **SEC**, **FCA**, and **Brazilian Securities Commission (CVM)**, collaborated to investigate insider trades linked to executives at Petrobras. Forensic investigators analysed trades executed in offshore accounts, uncovering a global network of insiders. This international cooperation, combined with forensic data-sharing agreements, was critical in prosecuting the offenders.

Chapter 11

Landmark Insider Trading Judgments

Insider trading has been the focus of some of the most high-profile legal battles in global financial markets. These cases have not only shaped the enforcement landscape but also influenced **corporate governance practices**, regulatory approaches, and the public's perception of market integrity. This provides an in-depth analysis of key insider trading judgments, including **SEBI vs. Rakesh Agarwal**, **U.S. vs. Rajat Gupta**, and the **Martha Stewart case**. We explore the **forensic evidence**, **legal precedents**, and the **global impact** of these rulings on insider trading laws and enforcement practices.

1. SEBI vs. Rakesh Agarwal: Defining the Legal Landscape in India

The **SEBI vs. Rakesh Agarwal** case is considered a landmark in India's insider trading jurisprudence, setting critical legal precedents and shaping the regulatory framework for market conduct. This case tested the boundaries of **insider trading laws** in India and highlighted the complexity of prosecuting insider trading.

The Case: A Brief Overview

Rakesh Agarwal, the managing director of **DSQ Software Ltd.**, was accused of trading shares based on **material non-public information (MNPI)** related to the company's acquisition of a large U.S. software company. Agarwal had privileged access to information about the acquisition and used it to trade shares in the company, both for personal gain and through proxies.

Forensic Evidence and Investigation

SEBI's investigation into Agarwal's trading activities relied heavily on **forensic data** from trading records, **email trails**, and **phone call logs**. SEBI's **forensic analysts** scrutinized the **timing of trades** in relation to corporate announcements and market activity. One of the most significant pieces of evidence was the correlation between **Agarwal's communication** with brokers and the corresponding spike in trading volumes in DSQ Software's stock before the public announcement of the acquisition. SEBI used this forensic evidence to establish that Agarwal traded based on MNPI.

- **Metadata Analysis**: SEBI's forensic team analyzed metadata from emails and phone logs, confirming the precise timing of communications between Agarwal and external brokers. This helped SEBI prove that Agarwal provided insider information and profited from the upcoming acquisition.

Legal Judgment and Impact

The judgment against Agarwal resulted in a **heavy fine** and a **lifetime ban** from trading on Indian stock exchanges, marking one of the most severe penalties ever imposed by SEBI at that time. The case underscored SEBI's commitment to using **forensic technology** to build strong insider trading cases and its ability to pursue both **civil and criminal actions** in such matters.

Impact on India's Insider Trading Policies

- **Strengthening of SEBI Regulations**: The outcome of this case prompted SEBI to revise and strengthen its **Prohibition of Insider Trading Regulations (1992)**, which later evolved into the more stringent **2015 regulations**. The judgment emphasized the need for **comprehensive surveillance systems** and **real-time monitoring** of trading activities, resulting in the development of SEBI's **Integrated Market Surveillance System (IMSS)**.

- **Corporate Governance**: This case heightened the focus on corporate governance standards in India. Public companies were required to establish stricter **insider trading policies** and **compliance mechanisms** to prevent such violations in the future.

2. U.S. vs. Rajat Gupta: Insider Trading and Corporate Governance Failures

The **U.S. vs. Rajat Gupta** case is one of the most significant insider trading prosecutions in American corporate history, not only because of the prominence of the defendant but also because it highlighted the critical failures in **corporate governance** and the responsibilities of **board members**. Gupta, a former managing director of **McKinsey & Company** and board member of **Goldman Sachs**, was accused of sharing **MNPI** with hedge fund manager **Raj Rajaratnam**.

The Case: A Brief Overview

Rajat Gupta, who held prestigious positions on the boards of companies like **Goldman Sachs** and **Procter & Gamble**, was found guilty of sharing inside information with Rajaratnam, the head of **Galleon Group**. The information related to Goldman Sachs' strategic moves during the financial crisis, including an emergency $5 billion investment from **Warren Buffett's Berkshire Hathaway**, which Rajaratnam used to make illegal trades.

Forensic Evidence and Investigation

The SEC and the **Department of Justice (DOJ)** relied on a wide range of forensic evidence, including **wiretaps**, **email records**, and **trading data**, to build their case against Gupta. Forensic investigators used **digital forensics** to recover deleted emails and trace **phone call metadata** that showed a pattern of communication between Gupta and Rajaratnam, particularly around key corporate events.

- **Wiretaps**: Wiretaps were critical in this case, providing direct evidence of Gupta discussing insider information with Rajaratnam. The recorded phone conversations played a crucial role in proving the **intent** behind Gupta's actions, as they revealed that Gupta had provided MNPI just minutes before Rajaratnam executed significant trades.

- **Forensic Trading Analysis**: The SEC's **Market Information Data Analytics System (MIDAS)** was employed to track the exact timing of trades made by Galleon Group following Gupta's tips. This **trade execution analysis** demonstrated how Rajaratnam leveraged the information to make millions of dollars in illegal profits.

Legal Judgment and Impact

Gupta was sentenced to **two years in prison**, a **$5 million fine**, and a permanent ban from serving as an officer or director of any public company. This case was a landmark in holding board members accountable for insider trading, highlighting the **fiduciary duties** of corporate leaders.

Impact on U.S. Insider Trading Policies

- **Boardroom Oversight**: This case significantly influenced the way corporations approach **boardroom ethics** and **compliance training** for board members. Corporate governance standards were tightened to ensure that board members are more vigilant about handling sensitive information.

- **Whistleblower Incentives**: In the wake of this case, the SEC increased its efforts to promote its **Whistleblower Program**, which rewards individuals for reporting insider trading and other securities violations. The use of forensic evidence and whistleblower tips has since become an integral part of insider trading enforcement in the U.S.

3. The Martha Stewart Case: Insider Trading Prosecution in the Public Eye

The prosecution of **Martha Stewart** is one of the most widely publicized insider trading cases in history. Although Stewart was not charged with the actual act of insider trading but rather for **obstruction of justice** and **lying to federal**

investigators, the case highlighted how **high-profile individuals** could be involved in insider trading scandals.

The Case: A Brief Overview

Martha Stewart, the founder of **Martha Stewart Living Omnimedia**, was accused of insider trading after selling shares of **ImClone Systems** based on a tip she received from her broker regarding the company's pending FDA rejection of a cancer drug. Stewart's close relationship with ImClone's CEO, **Sam Waksal**, further raised suspicion about her trading activities.

Forensic Evidence and Investigation

The SEC's case against Stewart heavily relied on **communication logs** and **forensic financial records**. Stewart's **phone records** showed calls between her and her broker, where she allegedly received a tip to sell her shares just before the FDA announced the rejection, causing ImClone's stock price to plummet.

- **Financial Forensics**: The SEC traced Stewart's sale of **3,928 shares** of ImClone stock, which took place just days before the public announcement. Forensic accountants reviewed her **trading history** and linked the timing of her trades directly to the information provided by her broker.

- **Obstruction of Justice**: Stewart's efforts to cover up her actions became central to the case. Forensic analysis of **emails and call logs** revealed attempts to mislead investigators, leading to her conviction not for insider trading but for **conspiracy, obstruction of justice, and making false statements**.

Legal Judgment and Impact

Stewart was sentenced to **five months in prison**, five months of home confinement, and a **$30,000 fine**. Despite the relatively short sentence, the case had a major impact on **public perceptions** of insider trading and the role of prominent figures in maintaining market integrity.

Impact on Global Insider Trading Policies

- **Heightened Public Awareness**: The Stewart case brought insider trading into the public eye in a way few cases had before. It underscored the idea that **celebrity status** does not exempt individuals from the law and reinforced the importance of **equal enforcement** of insider trading rules, regardless of an individual's prominence.

- **Enhanced Broker Accountability**: As a result of the case, regulators focused more on the **responsibilities of brokers** and financial advisors in preventing insider trading. Stewart's broker was also charged, and the case influenced the way brokers handle sensitive information and communicate with their clients.

4. Impact of These Judgments on Global Insider Trading Policies

The landmark cases discussed above have had far-reaching effects on insider trading enforcement and policies globally. They highlight the importance of **forensic evidence**, the role of **corporate governance**, and the use of **wiretaps and whistleblowers** in building insider trading cases.

Global Regulatory Cooperation and Cross-Border Enforcement

As a result of these cases, regulators around the world, including SEBI, the SEC, and the **Financial Conduct Authority (FCA)** in the U.K., have increased their cooperation through **Memoranda of Understanding (MoUs)** and global bodies such as the **International Organization of Securities Commissions (IOSCO)**. These agreements facilitate the exchange of evidence, joint investigations, and coordinated enforcement actions in cross-border insider trading cases.

Increased Use of Forensic Technologies

The reliance on **digital forensics**, **trade data analytics**, and **wiretaps** in these landmark cases has influenced how insider trading cases are prosecuted worldwide. Regulators now routinely use sophisticated forensic tools to analyze trading patterns, reconstruct communication trails, and recover deleted or hidden evidence.

Corporate Governance Reforms

The **U.S. vs. Rajat Gupta** and **SEBI vs. Rakesh Agarwal** cases have spurred significant reforms in corporate governance. Public companies now have stronger **insider trading policies** in place, requiring board members and executives to adhere to stricter standards of confidentiality and transparency.

- **Global Standards for Insider Trading Policies**: The aftermath of these cases has led to a global push for more robust **insider trading compliance programs**. Multinational corporations, particularly those listed on multiple exchanges, are required to implement policies that align with the most stringent international standards, including **pre-clearance of trades, blackout periods**, and **whistleblower protection programs**.

Conclusion

These landmark insider trading cases have reshaped the regulatory landscape across the globe, influencing how insider trading is detected, prosecuted, and prevented. From the use of forensic technologies in **SEBI vs. Rakesh Agarwal**, to the corporate governance lessons learned in **U.S. vs. Rajat Gupta**, and the public awareness raised by the **Martha Stewart case**, each judgment has left a lasting impact on how insider trading is viewed and regulated. As global regulators continue to cooperate and enhance their forensic capabilities, the fight against insider trading will only become more sophisticated, ensuring that markets remain fair and transparent for all participants.

Chapter 12

Notorious Insider Trading SCAMs

Insider trading scams have significantly shaped global financial markets, regulatory frameworks, and enforcement mechanisms. These high-profile cases underscore how **material non-public information (MNPI)** can be exploited by individuals within complex networks, often involving advanced market manipulation and corporate governance failures. Some of the most notorious insider trading scandals, such as the Harshad Mehta Scam, Raj Rajaratnam's Galleon Group case, and the Enron debacle, have shaped financial markets in profound ways. These cases not only highlight the ethical breaches at the heart of insider trading but also provide insight into the forensic tools and legal frameworks used to detect and prosecute such crimes. Additionally, these events have left a lasting impact on insider trading regulations globally, prompting more stringent rules and enforcement mechanisms. Technological advancements have also played a key role, enabling regulators to enhance surveillance and enforcement efforts, ensuring that markets operate more transparently and fairly.

1. The Harshad Mehta Scam: Changing the Face of Indian Financial Markets

The **Harshad Mehta Scam** of 1992 remains a seminal case in India's financial history, significantly shaping the evolution of **capital market regulations** and highlighting systemic vulnerabilities that were exploited through both **insider trading** and market manipulation. While the scam primarily involved fraudulent financial instruments, insider trading played a pivotal role in driving up stock prices based on **privileged information**.

The Scam: A Complex Web of Financial Manipulation

Hars had Mehta, a renowned stockbroker, used a scheme involving **fraudulent banking receipts (BRs)** and government securities to funnel money into the stock market. Mehta leveraged this capital to artificially inflate the prices of stocks such as **ACC**, **Reliance**, and **Tata Steel**. By creating a perception of market confidence and driving up prices based on manipulated liquidity, Mehta exploited the market's **price discovery mechanism**.

Insider Trading Aspect of the Scam

The crux of Mehta's insider trading involvement stemmed from his access to **non-public information** regarding the liquidity positions of banks and government securities, which allowed him to trade large volumes of shares before critical market movements. This strategy helped him execute trades in a manner that capitalized on **asymmetric information** to manipulate the market.

Forensic Evidence and Investigation Techniques

Forensic auditors from the **Reserve Bank of India (RBI)** and SEBI employed a series of sophisticated forensic methods to investigate Mehta's network of trades and financial transactions. The investigators utilized **forensic accounting** to trace the illegal transfers of money between banks and stockbrokers, demonstrating how Mehta misappropriated funds intended for government securities to fuel his stock market manipulation.

- **Advanced Transaction Analytics**: Investigators performed deep forensic analysis on the **movement of BRs**, identifying the misuse of banking systems to divert funds into stock purchases. These forensic audits provided a detailed financial trail that linked Mehta's illegal banking activities with the abnormal spikes in stock prices.

- **Market Surveillance Systems**: SEBI utilized its early versions of **market surveillance software** to detect unusual trading volumes in key stocks. By analysing **time-stamped trades** and mapping them against market-moving news and liquidity injections, SEBI was able to identify patterns of insider trading, including Mehta's orchestration of stock price manipulation.

Legal Outcomes and Regulatory Impact

The prosecution of Harshad Mehta resulted in multiple convictions, including a **five-year prison sentence** and a heavy financial penalty. The case also led to extensive reforms in India's financial markets, including the establishment of the **National Stock Exchange (NSE)**, the introduction of **screen-**

based trading, and the **Depositories Act** to dematerialize securities and improve transparency.

Regulatory Changes:

- **SEBI's Enhanced Powers**: The Harshad Mehta scam led to a massive overhaul of SEBI's regulatory authority, granting it greater oversight and enforcement powers to monitor insider trading and market manipulation. SEBI's **Prohibition of Insider Trading Regulations (1992)** were expanded, setting the foundation for future regulations like the **2015 Insider Trading Regulations**.

- **Adoption of Technological Surveillance**: The scandal accelerated the adoption of electronic trading systems and **real-time market surveillance**, enabling SEBI to detect abnormal trading patterns and potential insider trading through its **Integrated Market Surveillance System (IMSS)** and **Trade Analytics Software (TAS)**.

2. Raj Rajaratnam and Galleon Group: The Role of Wiretaps in Prosecution

The **Galleon Group** insider trading scandal, orchestrated by hedge fund manager **Raj Rajaratnam**, is one of the most complex and far-reaching insider trading cases in U.S. history. This case redefined the role of **wiretaps** and digital forensics in financial crime investigations and highlighted the **collusion between corporate insiders** and hedge funds in exploiting MNPI.

The Scam: A Network of Insider Trading

Rajaratnam, the founder of Galleon Group, coordinated a network of corporate insiders across industries, including technology, **pharmaceuticals**, and **financial services**, to access MNPI. This insider information was provided by executives at firms such as **Intel**, **Goldman Sachs**, and **Google**, which Rajaratnam used to execute highly profitable trades. The total illegal profits amassed from these trades exceeded **$70 million**.

Forensic Techniques and Wiretap Evidence

The **SEC** and **Department of Justice (DOJ)** employed **wiretaps** as a breakthrough investigative tool, gathering direct evidence of insider trading communications between Rajaratnam and his network of informants. The use of wiretaps in this case marked the first time such techniques were deployed on a large scale in financial crime investigations.

- **Wiretap Technology**: Wiretaps provided **real-time audio recordings** of Rajaratnam discussing MNPI with corporate insiders. This was critical in proving the intent behind his trades, as the wiretaps recorded specific instances where executives like **Rajat Gupta** (former Goldman Sachs board member) disclosed information about impending deals and quarterly earnings.

- **Forensic Trade Data Analysis**: The SEC's **Market Information Data Analytics System (MIDAS)** was pivotal in tracking the timing and execution of Rajaratnam's trades. Forensic analysts used MIDAS to correlate the **precise timestamps of trades** with the MNPI shared in wiretapped conversations, revealing how Rajaratnam executed trades within minutes of receiving insider information.

Legal Outcomes and Sentencing

Rajaratnam was sentenced to **11 years in federal prison** and fined **$92.8 million**, making it one of the longest prison sentences for insider trading in U.S. history. His conviction marked a turning point in the use of **wiretaps** and sophisticated **trade surveillance systems** to combat insider trading.

Global Impact and Legal Precedents:

- **Increased Regulatory Scrutiny on Hedge Funds**: The Galleon case prompted regulators worldwide to impose stricter compliance requirements on hedge funds, particularly around **information barriers** and the use of **expert networks** that may provide access to MNPI.

- **Adoption of Wiretaps in Financial Crime Investigations**: The success of wiretaps in the Rajaratnam case encouraged other jurisdictions, including the **Financial Conduct Authority (FCA)** in the U.K. and **SEBI** in India, to consider similar surveillance techniques for insider trading investigations.

3. The Enron Scandal: How Insider Trading Contributed to Corporate Collapse

The **Enron scandal** represents a devastating example of **corporate fraud** and **insider trading** that led to one of the largest bankruptcies in U.S. history. While Enron's collapse was driven by widespread accounting fraud, insider trading played a significant role as executives sought to profit from their inside knowledge of the company's impending downfall.

The Scam: Corporate Fraud and Market Deception

Enron executives, including **Jeffrey Skilling** (CEO) and **Andrew Fastow** (CFO), used complex **accounting schemes** involving **special purpose entities (SPEs)** to hide debt and inflate profits. As Enron's financial troubles mounted, executives began selling their shares based on their knowledge of the company's true financial state, even as they publicly encouraged investors to buy more stock.

Forensic Techniques and Insider Trading Evidence

The forensic investigation into Enron's collapse uncovered a vast web of insider trading. Executives liquidated millions of dollars' worth of stock while assuring the public that the company was in good health.

- **Forensic Accounting**: Investigators used **forensic accounting** techniques to unravel Enron's complex financial statements, tracing funds through various off-balance-sheet SPEs. This forensic audit revealed that while the company was hiding billions in debt, key executives were selling their shares based on MNPI, avoiding substantial personal losses.

- **Transaction Data Forensics**: Forensic analysts examined the **timing of stock sales** by Enron executives, demonstrating that they had sold large volumes of shares just before negative financial reports were released. This evidence was combined with **email trails** and **internal memos** that showed executives knew about the company's dire financial situation long before the public was made aware.

Legal Outcomes and Sentencing

Multiple Enron executives were convicted of **fraud** and **insider trading**. CEO Jeffrey Skilling was sentenced to **24 years in prison**, and CFO Andrew Fastow received a **six-year sentence**. The Enron scandal led to the **Sarbanes-Oxley Act (2002)**, which introduced stricter **corporate governance** and **financial reporting** standards in the U.S.

Global Regulatory Reforms:

- **Sarbanes-Oxley Act (SOX)**: Enron's collapse prompted the passage of SOX, which requires executives to certify the accuracy of financial statements and imposes restrictions on insider trading during **blackout periods**. This act has become a global model for corporate governance reform.

- **Strengthened Whistleblower Protections**: The Enron scandal also led to enhanced whistleblower protections under SOX, providing legal safeguards for employees who report insider trading or corporate fraud.

4. Lessons Learned from Major Insider Trading Cases

1. The Evolution of Forensic Technology in Insider Trading Prosecutions

The use of **forensic technology** has become indispensable in detecting and prosecuting insider trading. Techniques like **wiretaps, trade data analytics,** and **forensic accounting** have revolutionized how regulators uncover and build airtight cases against insider traders. These advancements ensure that regulators can track trading patterns down to **microsecond**

precision, correlate trades with communications, and recover deleted or encrypted data.

2. The Role of Cross-Border Cooperation

Insider trading scams, such as **Rajaratnam's Galleon Group** and **Enron**, have demonstrated the need for **cross-border regulatory cooperation**. Global regulators, including SEBI, the SEC, and the FCA, now regularly collaborate to share **market surveillance data**, enhance **forensic investigations**, and pursue cross-border enforcement actions under frameworks like the **IOSCO Multilateral Memorandum of Understanding (MMoU)**.

3. Strengthened Corporate Governance and Compliance

Each of these scandals has emphasized the importance of **corporate governance**, leading to the implementation of more robust **compliance programs** to monitor insider trading, including the adoption of **pre-clearance of trades**, **trading blackout periods**, and **insider trading monitoring systems** at the board and executive levels.

Conclusion

These notorious insider trading scams illustrate the far-reaching impact that unethical trading practices can have on financial markets, corporate governance, and investor confidence. The evolution of **forensic technologies**, **legal frameworks**, and **global cooperation** has made it increasingly difficult for insider traders to operate undetected. As a result, regulatory bodies are now better equipped to maintain **market integrity** and hold those responsible for market manipulation accountable.

Chapter 13

Eye-Opening Insights: Why Insider Traders Sell Stocks

The motivation behind insider trading goes beyond mere access to **material non-public information (MNPI)**. The decision to sell stocks, especially by corporate insiders, is driven by a mix of **psychological, financial, and behavioural factors**. This chapter examines why insider traders are motivated to sell stocks, focusing on the influence of **greed, fear, ego**, corporate incentives such as **stock buybacks**, the impact of **financial pressures**, and **market cycles**, along with an exploration of how **behavioural economics** plays into insider trading dynamics. This in-depth analysis sheds light on the underlying drivers behind insider sales and what regulators should be aware of when identifying potential insider trading activities.

1. Psychological Factors Behind Insider Trading: Greed, Fear, and Ego

Psychological factors are often at the core of insider trading decisions. Insiders are not just driven by the financial gains from selling stocks based on privileged information; their decisions are influenced by emotional and cognitive biases such as **greed**, **fear**, and **ego**. Understanding these psychological factors provides insight into why insiders may engage in unethical or illegal trading behaviour.

Greed: The Desire for Excessive Gains

Greed is one of the primary motivators for insider trading. Insiders, who possess MNPI, often feel the **temptation to capitalize on their access** to confidential information to maximize personal wealth. The allure of fast, significant financial returns often outweighs the risks of prosecution, especially in markets where **regulatory enforcement** might seem weak or underdeveloped.

- **Excessive Optimism Bias**: Insiders may overestimate their ability to profit from MNPI without being caught, leading to risky and unethical decisions. This bias is often reinforced by **past successes** in trading, creating a **self-reinforcing cycle** where greed and overconfidence drive further violations.

- **Herd Mentality Among Executives**: In some corporate cultures, insider trading becomes normalized as a result of **peer behaviour**. If top executives frequently engage in the sale of stocks based on inside information, lower-level insiders may feel justified in mimicking their actions, perpetuating a culture of **market abuse**.

Fear: Loss Aversion and Risk Management

While greed drives insider trading for profit, **fear**—particularly **loss aversion**—plays an equally powerful role. Loss aversion refers to the psychological phenomenon where individuals prefer to avoid losses rather than achieve gains. In the context of insider trading, insiders may sell stocks based on

MNPI to **avoid personal financial losses** when they anticipate that bad news will soon be disclosed to the public.

- **Loss Aversion in Declining Markets**: During periods of economic uncertainty or **bear markets**, insiders who anticipate negative earnings announcements, regulatory actions, or market disruptions are more likely to sell shares to protect themselves from significant losses. This fear-based trading, driven by MNPI, can create **false market signals**, leading to **panic selling** among uninformed investors.

- **Overreaction to Short-Term Market Fluctuations**: Insiders may also sell stocks out of fear of short-term market volatility, believing that the market will penalize their company's stock price more severely than justified. This short-term perspective, driven by **overconfidence** in their predictive abilities, can exacerbate market fluctuations.

Ego: The Desire for Control and Power

Ego, particularly a sense of **superiority** or **invincibility**, is a crucial factor in insider trading decisions. Many insiders believe they possess **superior knowledge** and insight, fuelling a sense of **control over market outcomes**. This **hubris** leads some insiders to believe they are immune to detection or that they can manipulate the system without consequences.

- **Ego-Driven Risk-Taking**: Insiders with inflated egos are more likely to take significant risks, selling large volumes of stock based on MNPI. This risk-taking is often reinforced by a **track record of past success**, creating a belief that they are invincible and can outsmart regulators.

- **Control Over Market Perceptions**: Insiders with ego-driven motivations may use stock sales to signal their control over a company's financial destiny, influencing both internal stakeholders and market participants. By selling shares at strategic moments, these insiders believe they can shape market sentiment and reinforce their dominance over corporate outcomes.

2. Corporate Incentives and Stock Buybacks: Legal and Ethical Questions

Corporate incentives, particularly through **stock buybacks**, can create fertile ground for insider trading. While **stock buybacks** are a legal corporate strategy to boost **earnings per share (EPS)** and increase shareholder value, insiders may exploit buybacks for personal gain. This section explores the **intersection of corporate incentives** and insider trading, highlighting the **legal and ethical implications**.

Stock Buybacks and Timing of Insider Sales

Stock buybacks are often announced when companies believe their stock is undervalued, signalling confidence in future growth. However, insiders with knowledge of upcoming buybacks may pre-emptively sell their shares, knowing that the buyback will drive up the stock price, thereby allowing them to maximize their profits.

- **Legal vs. Ethical Dilemma**: While stock buybacks are legal, the **timing of insider sales** around such announcements raises significant **ethical questions**. In many jurisdictions, insiders are prohibited from trading in **blackout periods**, which occur before earnings announcements or buybacks. However, enforcement of these blackout periods can be inconsistent, allowing insiders to exploit legal loopholes.

- **Earnings Management and Buybacks**: Insiders may also time their stock sales to coincide with **earnings management practices**. By artificially inflating stock prices through buybacks and strategic earnings announcements, insiders can sell shares at inflated prices, profiting at the expense of **uninformed investors**.

Incentive-Based Compensation and Stock Options

Corporate executives are often compensated through **stock options** and other **equity-based incentives**, aligning their interests with shareholder value. However, these compensation packages can create **perverse incentives** for insiders to sell their shares based on MNPI to secure personal financial gains.

- **Options Vesting and Insider Trading**: Insiders are often required to hold their shares for a certain period before exercising stock options. However, once these options **vest**, insiders may sell stocks ahead of **negative earnings announcements** or **market downturns**, capitalizing on their MNPI to avoid personal financial losses.

- **Executive Bonuses Tied to Stock Performance**: Executives whose bonuses are tied to stock price performance may manipulate **stock buybacks**, share sales, and earnings announcements to ensure their bonuses are maximized. This creates an environment where **corporate ethics** are undermined, and the focus shifts from long-term growth to short-term personal gain.

3. The Role of Financial Pressure and Market Cycles

Financial pressures—both personal and corporate—play a significant role in insider trading activities. Insiders may be compelled to sell stocks due to **financial stress**, particularly during certain **market cycles**. This section explores how **financial pressures**, both internal and external, influence insider trading behaviour.

Personal Financial Stress and Insider Trading

Executives facing **personal financial challenges**, such as **debt, divorce settlements**, or **liquidity constraints**, are more likely to engage in **desperation-driven insider trading**. In these cases, insiders use MNPI to **liquidate shares** quickly and at favorable prices, attempting to resolve their financial crises before adverse news is made public.

- **Executive Debt and Margin Calls**: Many corporate insiders hold substantial portions of their wealth in company stock, often purchased on **margin** (using borrowed funds). During periods of market volatility, these insiders may face **margin calls**, forcing them to sell their shares based on MNPI to cover their debts.

- **Behavioural Pressure**: **Behavioural finance** suggests that insiders, under financial stress, are more likely to engage in irrational decision-making, such as selling stocks at inopportune times or ignoring ethical boundaries in pursuit of personal liquidity.

Market Cycles and Timing of Insider Sales

Insider trading patterns often correlate with **market cycles**, particularly during **bear markets**, **recessions**, or **financial crises**. Insiders, with early access to MNPI, often react to market downturns by selling shares to avoid significant losses.

- **Behavioural Timing in Market Cycles**: During market downturns, insiders may engage in **panic selling** or attempt to time the market based on non-public knowledge of upcoming earnings or broader economic conditions. This behaviour disrupts the normal **price discovery** process, leading to **market inefficiencies** and further volatility.

- **Counter-Cyclical Insider Trading**: Some insiders engage in **counter-cyclical trading** by selling shares in **rising markets**, anticipating corrections based on MNPI about the company's actual financial health. This allows them to lock in gains before the broader market adjusts to adverse information.

4. Behavioural Economics in Insider Trading

Behavioural economics offers a deeper understanding of why insiders make seemingly irrational decisions when trading on MNPI. By examining cognitive biases and heuristics, behavioral economics helps explain the often contradictory and self-destructive nature of insider trading.

Overconfidence and Illusion of Control

Many insiders suffer from **overconfidence bias**, where they believe they can successfully time the market and profit from insider trading without being caught. This sense of control leads to riskier trading behaviour, often exacerbating the impact of MNPI-driven sales on the market.

- **Illusion of Control**: Insiders often believe they have more control over market outcomes than they actually do. This illusion can drive them to **overestimate** their ability to influence stock prices through insider trading, leading to more significant sales or more frequent trading.

Anchoring and Availability Bias

Anchoring occurs when insiders fixate on specific price points, often based on past stock performance, and fail to adjust their expectations based on new information. **Availability bias** may cause insiders to rely too heavily on **recent events**, such as a previous successful insider trade, and ignore the **long-term risks** associated with repeated trading on MNPI.

- **Anchoring in Stock Sales**: Insiders may anchor their decision to sell stocks at specific price levels, even if those levels are inflated by **market manipulation** or **buyback schemes**. This distorted decision-making can lead to significant financial gains in the short term but can also increase the likelihood of regulatory scrutiny.

Herd Behaviour in Corporate Insider Networks

In some cases, insider trading can become a **collective behaviour**, driven by **herd mentality**. Insiders may trade based on MNPI because they see their peers doing the same, reinforcing unethical behaviour within **executive networks**.

- **Social Norms and Peer Influence**: When corporate insiders see their colleagues profiting from MNPI, they may be more likely to follow suit, driven by social norms and the desire to achieve similar financial gains. This herd behaviour creates a **network effect** of insider trading, making detection and prosecution more challenging for regulators.

Conclusion

Insider trading is driven by a complex mix of **psychological**, **corporate**, and **market-based factors**. Greed, fear, and ego often cloud the judgment of corporate insiders, leading them to sell stocks based on MNPI. Corporate structures, particularly **stock buybacks** and **incentive-based compensation**, further exacerbate these unethical behaviours, creating an environment ripe for market manipulation. **Behavioural economics** offers valuable insights into how cognitive biases influence insider trading decisions, providing a framework for understanding the seemingly irrational behaviour of market insiders.

As regulators continue to adopt advanced **forensic tools** and behavioural monitoring techniques, the fight against insider trading will require deeper understanding not only of **market mechanics** but also of the human behaviours that drive illegal activities. By recognizing the patterns and motivations behind insider stock sales, regulatory bodies can refine their **surveillance** and **enforcement** strategies, maintaining **market integrity** and protecting **investor confidence**.

Chapter 14

Insider Trading and Blockchain

Blockchain technology is revolutionizing how financial systems function, particularly in terms of transparency, security, and traceability. In the context of **insider trading**, blockchain can serve as a game-changer by providing regulators with tools to better monitor and detect illegal activities in stock markets. This chapter explores the significant role of blockchain in transforming market transparency, how **smart contracts** and decentralized systems can improve insider trading detection, the potential applications of blockchain in stock market surveillance, and the regulatory perspectives on this emerging technology.

Blockchain: A New Paradigm for Market Transparency and Auditable Trading

Blockchain technology has emerged as a transformative tool for enhancing transparency, security, and accountability in the financial markets. Blockchain is a **Distributed Ledger Technology** (DLT) that records transactions in a secure, decentralized manner, providing an immutable audit trail for all activities.

Blockchain's Role in Preventing Insider Trading:

- **Real-time auditable transactions**: Blockchain records all transactions transparently, allowing regulators to access an immutable record of every trade. This reduces the risk of tampering or post-trade manipulation.

- **Smart contracts**: These self-executing contracts can automate certain trading activities, ensuring compliance with insider trading regulations without human intervention.

- **Elimination of intermediaries**: Blockchain reduces the need for brokers and other middlemen, cutting down on opportunities for **information leakage**.

Major stock exchanges, including **Nasdaq** and the **Australian Securities Exchange (ASX)**, are exploring blockchain for trading and post-trade activities, which could revolutionize how insider trading is monitored and detected.

In India, **SEBI** is investigating the use of blockchain to improve transparency in market transactions and reduce the likelihood of market manipulation, making it a powerful future tool in the regulator's arsenal against insider trading.

1. How Blockchain Technology is Transforming Market Transparency

Blockchain's distributed ledger technology (DLT) introduces a **trust-less** and **transparent system** that fundamentally changes how financial markets operate. This decentralization creates a system where every transaction is **traceable, immutable**, and **visible to authorized parties**. By recording every transaction on a public or private blockchain, the potential for illegal insider trading activity can be significantly reduced.

Decentralization: Eliminating the Need for Intermediaries

Blockchain operates on a **peer-to-peer (P2P)** network, which eliminates the need for intermediaries such as brokers or clearinghouses. This decentralized structure enhances market transparency because **every participant in the network** holds a copy of the transaction ledger, making it nearly impossible for an insider to conduct unauthorized trades without leaving a trace.

- **Market Transparency**: In traditional markets, clearinghouses and brokers control transaction records, creating potential blind spots for regulators. Blockchain allows for **real-time visibility** into every trade, meaning that regulatory authorities can monitor trades directly, rather than relying on third-party reporting systems.

- **Immutable Records**: The immutability of blockchain means that once a transaction is logged, it cannot be altered or deleted. For insider trading, this is particularly important because any trades made using **material non-public information (MNPI)** would be permanently recorded and available for future audit. This creates a **transparent audit trail** that can be used as evidence in investigations.

Distributed Ledger Technology: Enhancing Auditability and Accountability

In blockchain systems, the **distributed ledger** ensures that every transaction is copied across multiple nodes in the network. This distribution enhances **accountability** by creating a **tamper-**

proof audit trail that anyone with access to the blockchain can review.

- **Real-Time Auditability**: For regulators, the distributed nature of blockchain provides **real-time auditing** capabilities. Every trade executed on the blockchain is visible immediately, and regulators can track the flow of assets and information in near real-time. This makes it harder for insiders to manipulate the market or execute trades before public disclosure of MNPI.

- **Traceability**: Blockchain makes it easier to trace the origins of every trade, including the parties involved and the financial instruments used. In cases of suspected insider trading, investigators can trace each transaction from the insider back to the market and determine whether MNPI was used to influence the trade.

Case Example: Nasdaq's Linq Blockchain for Private Equity

Nasdaq's **Linq** blockchain technology provides an example of how blockchain can be used to enhance transparency in private equity trading. By issuing shares of private companies on a blockchain, Linq creates a **transparent ledger** where all equity transactions are visible to market participants and regulators. This transparency makes it harder for insiders to manipulate private stock prices for personal gain and offers regulators a clear audit trail for monitoring trades.

2. Using Blockchain to Monitor Insider Trades: Smart Contracts and Auditing

Blockchain technology offers not just transparency but also the ability to **automate compliance** and **enforce trading restrictions** through **smart contracts**. Smart contracts can be used to monitor insider trades, ensure compliance with regulations, and automatically report trades in real time to the relevant authorities. This section explores how smart contracts can be used to **prevent unauthorized insider trades** and improve **auditing** in stock markets.

Smart Contracts: Automating Insider Trade Compliance

Smart contracts are self-executing contracts with the terms of the agreement embedded directly into the blockchain. These contracts can be programmed to **enforce regulatory requirements**, such as **pre-clearance of trades** for insiders or **blackout periods** before earnings announcements.

- **Pre-Trade Authorization**: Smart contracts can be used to prevent insiders from executing trades unless the trade meets certain predefined conditions. For example, before an insider can sell shares, a smart contract could verify whether the trade complies with blackout periods or if it has been **pre-approved by the compliance department**. If the conditions are not met, the trade will not be executed.

- **Real-Time Regulatory Reporting**: Smart contracts can also automate the reporting of trades to regulatory bodies like the **SEC** or **SEBI**. When an insider executes a trade, the smart contract can automatically generate a **regulatory filing** (such as SEC Form 4) and send it to the appropriate authorities. This eliminates delays in reporting and ensures **real-time compliance**.

Decentralized Auditing and Compliance Systems

Blockchain allows for the creation of **decentralized auditing systems** where **all market participants**—from regulators to auditors—can access and verify trades without the need for intermediaries. This ensures that all trading activity is **continuously monitored** and that suspicious trades are flagged in real time.

- **Immutable Audits**: Blockchain creates an **immutable audit trail** where every trade, communication, and decision points are recorded. This makes it easier for auditors and regulators to detect patterns of **market manipulation** or insider trading. If a corporate insider attempts to execute an illegal trade, the **entire transaction history** will be available for review, providing forensic evidence for prosecution.

- **Continuous Compliance Monitoring**: Blockchain enables **real-time compliance monitoring**, meaning that the system continuously checks whether trades are executed within legal guidelines. Compliance officers can set up automated alerts for suspicious trading patterns, allowing regulators to take immediate action when necessary.

Case Example: Smart Contracts in Stock Tokenization

The **SIX Swiss Exchange** is using blockchain-based **tokenization** to digitize and trade securities on a blockchain. In this system, **smart contracts** automatically enforce compliance rules, ensuring that trades cannot be executed unless they meet regulatory requirements. This ensures that insider trades are **instantly transparent** and subject to real-time regulatory oversight, preventing abuse of MNPI.

3. Applications of Blockchain in Stock Market Surveillance

Blockchain's capabilities extend beyond smart contracts and auditing. It can also be used to improve **stock market surveillance**, allowing regulators to detect and investigate insider trading in real time. Blockchain's transparent architecture enables **continuous surveillance** of trades and patterns, making it an ideal tool for identifying insider trading activity.

Real-Time Monitoring of Trades and Market Behaviour

One of blockchain's most powerful applications is in **real-time market surveillance**. In a blockchain-based stock exchange, every transaction is visible to participants and regulators in real time, creating a system where any suspicious trades or patterns can be instantly flagged for review.

- **Anomaly Detection**: Using **machine learning algorithms** and **big data analytics**, regulators can analyse trading behaviour across the blockchain. By comparing trading patterns with historical data, these systems can detect **anomalies** such as **unusual trading volumes** before earnings reports or large sell-offs by insiders before bad news is announced.

- **Cross-Exchange Monitoring**: In today's global markets, insiders may attempt to evade detection by executing trades on **multiple exchanges** across jurisdictions. Blockchain can serve as a unified platform for monitoring trades across different stock exchanges in real time, enabling regulators to identify **cross-border insider trading** more easily.

Blockchain-Based Trade Attribution and Identity Verification

In cases of insider trading, one of the biggest challenges is identifying who is behind the trades. Blockchain's **identity verification** capabilities make it easier to link every trade to a specific person or entity.

- **Digital Identity Verification**: Through the use of **blockchain-based digital identities**, regulators can ensure that every trade is tied to a verified identity. This makes it more difficult for insiders to use intermediaries, shell companies, or anonymous trading accounts to execute trades without being detected.

- **Trade Attribution**: Blockchain provides a **clear attribution** for every trade, allowing regulators to track exactly who executed the trade, when it was executed, and what information was used to make the decision. This level of transparency greatly reduces the risk of **fraudulent trading** and makes enforcement easier.

Case Example: Overstock's tZERO Platform

tZERO, a blockchain-based trading platform developed by Overstock, allows for the issuance and trading of **tokenized securities**. All transactions on the platform are recorded on a **distributed ledger**, ensuring that every trade is traceable and compliant with regulatory requirements. This level of transparency and real-time surveillance could be used to prevent and detect insider trading activities more effectively.

4. Regulatory Perspectives on Blockchain-Enabled Financial Systems

While blockchain offers significant benefits in terms of **transparency** and **accountability**, its adoption in financial markets presents challenges for regulators. Financial regulatory bodies such as **SEBI**, the **SEC**, and the **FCA** are working to understand how blockchain can be integrated into existing regulatory frameworks while ensuring **market integrity** and protecting investors.

SEBI's Approach to Blockchain and Insider Trading

SEBI has been exploring the use of blockchain for **market surveillance** and improving transparency in India's stock markets. The regulator is particularly interested in how blockchain can be used to track **securities transactions** and enforce compliance in real time.

- **Blockchain for KYC Compliance**: One potential application SEBI is examining is the use of blockchain to improve **Know Your Customer (KYC)** processes. By integrating KYC data into a blockchain ledger, SEBI could ensure that every trader on the platform is verified, reducing the risk of **fraudulent or anonymous trades**.

- **Scalability and Legal Challenges**: SEBI has recognized that while blockchain offers significant benefits, there are still challenges related to **scalability** and **data privacy**. Additionally, the legal framework for **blockchain securities** is still in its infancy, and SEBI will need to create new regulations to address issues such as **smart contract enforceability** and **tokenized asset ownership**.

SEC's Regulatory Approach to Blockchain Securities

The **SEC** has taken a proactive approach in regulating blockchain-based securities, ensuring that these assets comply with **securities laws** and offering guidelines for blockchain platforms to operate legally.

- **Regulation of Tokenized Securities**: Under the **Howey Test**, the SEC has classified most blockchain-based assets as securities, meaning they must comply with existing regulations such as **Regulation SHO** and **Regulation ATS**. Blockchain platforms offering tokenized securities must register with the SEC as **Alternative Trading Systems (ATS)** and comply with securities trading rules.

- **Blockchain for Regulatory Oversight**: The SEC's **FinHub** division has been at the forefront of researching how blockchain can be used for **regulatory oversight**. Through blockchain, the SEC aims to create a system where every trade is **fully auditable** and **traceable** back to its source, reducing the risk of **market manipulation**.

FCA's Regulatory Sandbox for Blockchain Technologies

The **Financial Conduct Authority (FCA)** in the U.K. has taken a progressive stance on blockchain innovation through its **regulatory sandbox**, which allows companies to test new blockchain solutions under controlled conditions.

- **Blockchain in Market Surveillance**: Through its sandbox program, the FCA has encouraged the development of blockchain-based trading platforms designed to improve **market transparency** and **compliance monitoring**. These platforms use blockchain to create a **fully transparent ledger**, where regulators can monitor trades in real time and enforce compliance through automated systems.

- **Governance and Accountability**: The FCA has stressed the importance of ensuring that blockchain platforms have clear **governance structures** and **accountability mechanisms**. This is particularly important in the context of insider trading, where blockchain's transparency must be balanced with data privacy and market integrity concerns.

Conclusion

Blockchain technology holds immense potential to transform the detection and prosecution of **insider trading** by providing **transparent, tamper-proof** systems that enhance **market integrity**. Through the use of **smart contracts, decentralized auditing**, and **real-time surveillance,** blockchain can help regulators prevent and detect insider trading more effectively. However, the adoption of blockchain also presents regulatory challenges, requiring careful consideration of how to integrate blockchain-based systems into existing financial regulations.

Chapter 15

Criminal Aspects of Insider Trading

Insider trading has become one of the most aggressively prosecuted white-collar crimes across global financial markets. The complexity of proving insider trading, combined with the high-profile nature of many cases, has resulted in a series of **landmark prosecutions**. In this expanded section, we will delve deeper into notable criminal insider trading cases, including both high-profile cases and lesser-known but significant prosecutions. We'll examine how these cases were built, the role of **forensic evidence**, and their broader implications for market regulation.

1. SEBI vs. Rakesh Agrawal (India)

The Complaint

The **Securities and Exchange Board of India (SEBI)** initiated a complaint against **Rakesh Agrawal**, the managing director of **DSQ Software**, after discovering that he had executed trades based on **material non-public information (MNPI)**. The complaint outlined that Agrawal had knowledge of an upcoming acquisition of a U.S. software company and used this confidential information to trade shares in DSQ Software, thereby benefiting from the eventual market movement post-announcement.

Forensic Investigation and Detainment

SEBI's **Integrated Market Surveillance System (IMSS)** flagged suspicious trading activity in DSQ Software's shares, particularly large purchases executed by Agrawal and his associates. Forensic auditors were then assigned to investigate the trading patterns and review communication records, including phone calls and emails. The investigation revealed:

- **Timing of trades** that directly correlated with internal discussions about the acquisition.

- **Phone records** and **emails** showing Agrawal communicating with brokers shortly before executing trades.

SEBI's forensic team pieced together the evidence and corroborated it with **financial data** to demonstrate that Agrawal acted on inside knowledge. Based on the forensic report, SEBI filed for Agrawal's detainment and restricted his access to further trading on the stock exchange. Agrawal was subsequently detained pending a formal hearing.

Court's Consideration

In court, the following elements were considered:

- **MNPI Definition**: The court first confirmed whether the information about the acquisition qualified as MNPI under Indian securities law.

- **Breach of Fiduciary Duty**: As the managing director, Agrawal had a fiduciary duty to refrain from trading on non-public information. The court examined whether Agrawal had wilfully breached this duty.

- **Causality**: The court looked at the timing and volume of Agrawal's trades, matching them against market movements after the acquisition announcement to assess the extent of financial gain from his actions.

- The forensic evidence provided by SEBI was decisive, and the court imposed a **lifetime trading ban** and hefty fines, ruling that Agrawal had violated insider trading laws.

2. U.S. vs. Rajat Gupta (United States)

The Complaint

The **Securities and Exchange Commission (SEC)** and **Department of Justice (DOJ)** filed complaints against Rajat Gupta, a former board member of Goldman Sachs and Procter & Gamble, for passing MNPI to Raj Rajaratnam, the founder of Galleon Group. Gupta was accused of tipping Rajaratnam off with inside information about Goldman Sachs' earnings and the Warren Buffett investment, which Rajaratnam used to make illegal trades.

Forensic Investigation and Detainment

The investigation began after Rajaratnam's illegal trading was detected by the **SEC's Market Information Data Analytics System (MIDAS)**, which tracks market anomalies. Forensic analysis of **Rajaratnam's trading patterns** raised suspicion, and the SEC expanded its probe to include wiretaps authorized by the FBI.

- **Wiretap Evidence**: Over **2,000 conversations** were recorded between Rajaratnam and his associates. A key piece of evidence was a **recorded phone call** where Gupta informed Rajaratnam about a confidential board meeting at Goldman Sachs regarding Buffett's investment, just minutes before Rajaratnam placed trades.

- **Forensic Trading Data**: The forensic team correlated the **exact timing of phone calls** between Gupta and Rajaratnam with the subsequent execution of trades, proving a direct link between the MNPI and the illegal trades.

Gupta was not initially detained but was formally charged after the evidence from wiretaps and financial analysis was presented to a grand jury. His prestigious status made his trial highly publicized, and he voluntarily surrendered to authorities once the complaint was formally filed.

Court's Consideration

During the trial, the court focused on the following elements:

- **Fiduciary Responsibility**: Gupta, as a board member, had a fiduciary duty to maintain confidentiality regarding corporate matters. The court examined whether his actions constituted a wilful violation of this duty.

- **Wiretap Legality**: A significant part of the defense's argument revolved around the legality of using wiretaps in insider trading cases. The court ruled that the wiretaps were legal and critical to proving intent.

- **Intent**: The court placed heavy weight on proving Gupta's intent to pass MNPI for personal benefit or as a favour to Rajaratnam. The combination of wiretap evidence and trading patterns demonstrated clear intent.

Gupta was convicted on four counts of conspiracy and securities fraud, sentenced to **two years in prison**, and fined **$5 million**. The case set a legal precedent for using **wiretap evidence** in financial crime cases.

3. U.S. vs. Raj Rajaratnam and Galleon Group (United States)

The Complaint

The **SEC** and **DOJ** filed a massive complaint against **Raj Rajaratnam**, the founder of the **Galleon Group** hedge fund, for leading an insider trading ring involving multiple corporate insiders who provided MNPI. Rajaratnam's trades generated over **$70 million** in illegal profits, and the investigation uncovered a wide network of individuals tipping him off about corporate earnings, mergers, and acquisitions.

Forensic Investigation and Detainment

The **forensic investigation** began when unusual trading patterns associated with Galleon Group were flagged by the SEC's market surveillance systems. The investigation then expanded into one of the most comprehensive insider trading cases in history:

- **Wiretaps and Surveillance**: The **FBI authorized wiretaps**, capturing over **2,000 recorded conversations** where Rajaratnam was receiving insider tips. Forensic teams worked to analyze the timing of these calls in relation to stock trades.

- **Trade Analysis**: Forensic accountants and SEC analysts used MIDAS to match Rajaratnam's trades with corporate events, finding that he consistently traded just before public announcements, profiting from non-public information.

Rajaratnam was arrested and detained after the DOJ and SEC presented the wiretap evidence to a grand jury. He was charged with **multiple counts of securities fraud** and **conspiracy**. Given the volume of evidence, Rajaratnam's detainment was swift and followed by one of the largest insider trading trials ever conducted

Court's Consideration

The court's deliberation focused on:

- **Extent of the Fraud**: The scale of the insider trading scheme was unprecedented, involving numerous insiders from various companies. The court evaluated the systemic nature of Rajaratnam's network and the extent of illegal profits generated.

- **Use of Wiretaps**: The admissibility of wiretap evidence was heavily debated, but the court ruled it as crucial to proving **intent** and **coordination** among the defendants.

- **Pattern of Trading**: The forensic evidence provided a clear pattern linking insider tips with Rajaratnam's trading activities. This reinforced the court's view that Rajaratnam had systematically profited from MNPI.

Rajaratnam was convicted on **14 counts** of securities fraud and sentenced to **11 years in prison**, the longest sentence ever for insider trading in the U.S., along with a **$92.8 million fine**.

4. FCA vs. Martyn Dodgson (United Kingdom)

The Complaint

The **Financial Conduct Authority (FCA)** filed a complaint against **Martyn Dodgson**, a former director at **Deutsche Bank**, for passing MNPI about upcoming mergers and acquisitions to **James Sanders**, a trader at **Blue Index**. Dodgson and Sanders used this information to trade U.S. and U.K. stocks, generating significant profits from non-public knowledge.

Forensic Investigation and Detainment

The FCA's **Market Abuse Unit** initially detected unusual trading patterns in several U.S. and U.K. stocks, leading to a detailed forensic investigation:

- **Communications Analysis**: The FCA obtained **phone records** and **emails** that connected Dodgson to Sanders and their trading activities. The forensic team used these records to establish that Dodgson shared confidential information just before key trades were made.

- **Cross-Border Cooperation**: Given the international scope of the trading, the FCA collaborated with the **SEC** and **U.S. Department of Justice**, sharing forensic data to trace trades executed in U.S. markets. The cross-border nature of the scheme added complexity but also helped strengthen the case through joint investigative efforts.

Dodgson was arrested following a coordinated international operation, with both U.K. and U.S. authorities working together. The FCA's forensic report was pivotal in securing his detainment and eventual conviction.

Court's Consideration

In Dodgson's trial, the court considered the following:

- **Cross-Jurisdictional Evidence**: The court examined how evidence gathered in both the U.K. and the U.S. could be used cohesively to establish Dodgson's role in insider trading.

- **Forensic Communications Analysis**: Phone and email records were critical in proving Dodgson's communication with Sanders and others involved in the insider trading ring.

- **Market Manipulation**: The court reviewed how Dodgson's actions directly manipulated stock prices across multiple jurisdictions, leading to illegal gains.

Dodgson was sentenced to **4.5 years in prison**, marking one of the FCA's most significant victories in combating insider trading. This case set a benchmark for cross-border cooperation in insider trading enforcement.

5. The ImClone Systems and Martha Stewart Case (United States)

The Complaint

Martha Stewart became embroiled in the **ImClone insider trading scandal** after selling **3,928 shares** of **ImClone Systems** stock based on a tip from her broker, **Peter Bacanovic**, regarding the **FDA's upcoming rejection** of ImClone's cancer drug, **Erbitux**.

Forensic Investigation and Detainment

Although Stewart was not charged directly with insider trading, the SEC and FBI focused on her actions after the investigation began, including possible **obstruction of justice**:

- **Phone and Trading Records**: Forensic investigators reviewed phone records showing Stewart's communication with Bacanovic just before the trade. **Trade logs** indicated that Stewart sold her shares the day before ImClone's stock price plummeted.

- **Forensic Document Recovery**: The investigation also included **document recovery**, where altered notes from Bacanovic's office were uncovered. These notes were intended to show that Stewart had pre-authorized the sale, but forensic experts identified discrepancies that suggested post-facto alterations.

Stewart voluntarily surrendered to authorities once charges of obstruction and conspiracy were filed. Her prominent status meant that her detainment was highly scrutinized.

Court's Consideration

The court primarily focused on:

- **Obstruction of Justice**: Stewart's conviction centered on her efforts to mislead investigators rather than the insider trading itself. The forensic analysis of altered documents and conflicting testimonies played a key role in the obstruction charges.

- **Intent**: The prosecution argued that Stewart's intent was to cover up the reasons for her ImClone stock sale, and the forensic evidence supported this argument.

Stewart was convicted of conspiracy, obstruction of justice, and making false statements, resulting in a five-month prison sentence, five months of home confinement, and a $30,000 fine.

6. SEC vs. Matthew Kluger and Garrett Bauer (United States)

The Complaint

In one of the longest-running insider trading schemes uncovered by the SEC, **Matthew Kluger**, a corporate lawyer, and **Garrett Bauer**, a stock trader, engaged in insider trading for over **17 years**. Kluger accessed MNPI about corporate mergers from the law firms he worked at, passing the information to Bauer, who executed trades that generated **$37 million** in illegal profits.

Forensic Investigation and Detainment

The SEC's forensic team conducted a deep investigation into the long-running trading patterns:

- **Email and Trade Log Correlation**: Investigators recovered **emails** and **internal documents** from Kluger's law firms, showing that he had accessed confidential merger information. Forensic trade analysis then connected this information to trades placed by Bauer, matching the **timing of trades** with key corporate events.

- **Financial Forensics**: The forensic team traced the **flow of money** between Kluger and Bauer, proving that profits from illegal trades were laundered through a network of accounts. Forensic accountants built a comprehensive timeline of financial transactions that linked the two men.

Both Kluger and Bauer were arrested after the forensic evidence was presented to a grand jury. The SEC's complaint was bolstered by extensive documentary and trade evidence.

Court's Consideration

The court focused on:

- **Scope and Duration**: The **17-year span** of the insider trading scheme was unprecedented. The court examined how the defendants managed to avoid detection for so long, eventually concluding that their scheme's complexity did not mitigate the criminality of their actions.

- **Forensic Financial Analysis**: The **financial forensic evidence** was crucial in establishing the depth of the conspiracy and the extent of the illegal gains.

Both Kluger and Bauer were sentenced to **12 years in prison**, with the court noting the **systematic and prolonged nature** of the insider trading scheme.

Conclusion

The insider trading cases detailed in this chapter illustrate how **forensic evidence**, including **wiretaps, email trails**, and **financial analysis**, plays an essential role in modern insider trading prosecutions. Courts worldwide consider various factors, including **fiduciary breaches, intent,** and the **extent of financial gain**, in determining guilt and imposing penalties. These cases also highlight the importance of **cross-border cooperation**, as many insider trading schemes span multiple jurisdictions, requiring international regulatory collaboration.

Chapter 16

Practical Guidelines for Professionals and Investors

In today's fast-paced financial landscape, adhering to insider trading regulations is crucial for maintaining market integrity and avoiding severe penalties. A practical framework is essential for professionals, compliance officers, retail investors, and whistleblowers to protect themselves from the legal and financial risks associated with insider trading. This guide offers actionable **strategies, incorporating global best practices and leveraging the latest technological advancements**. By integrating robust compliance measures and legal safeguards, it equips market participants with the tools needed to navigate the complexities of insider trading regulations effectively.

1. Practical Framework for Professionals to Stay Compliant with Insider Trading Laws

1.1. Establishing a Clear Understanding of Material Non-Public Information (MNPI)

- **Training and Education**: Implement ongoing education programs on the definition of **MNPI**.

Professionals need to know what constitutes MNPI, including earnings reports, strategic acquisitions, boardroom decisions, and upcoming product launches.

- **Industry-Specific Guidelines**: Professionals in **pharmaceuticals**, **technology**, **banking**, and other sectors with rapid developments should receive tailored training, highlighting the specific types of information considered material within their industries.

Action Step:

- **Monthly Compliance Workshops**: Conduct workshops where real-world case studies are analyzed. Professionals should be trained on identifying MNPI and distinguishing between permissible and impermissible trades.

1.2. Pre-Trade Compliance Framework for Insiders

Corporate insiders should establish a **pre-clearance process** for all trades to ensure they are not acting on MNPI or trading during **blackout periods**.

- **Automated Pre-Clearance System**: Companies should implement an automated **pre-trade clearance system** that alerts compliance officers when an insider requests to trade company stock. This system should be linked to the company's **insider trading policy** and include checks for **blackout periods**, recent MNPI disclosures, and any pending corporate actions.

Action Step:

- **Pre-Clearance Request Form**: Create a digital form that corporate insiders must complete before making trades. This form should be automatically routed to compliance officers, and trading should not proceed until formal approval is granted.

1.3. Adoption of Rule 10b5-1 Trading Plans

In the United States, corporate insiders can adopt **Rule 10b5-1 plans**, which allow for pre-scheduled trades. By using these plans, insiders can mitigate the risk of **impropriety** because their trades are pre-planned, eliminating the suspicion that they acted on inside information.

- **Annual Review of 10b5-1 Plans**: Compliance officers should review Rule 10b5-1 plans annually to ensure the trading activity aligns with **regulatory requirements** and internal corporate policies.

Action Step:

- **Automation and Review of 10b5-1 Plans**: Utilize **AI-driven tools** to automatically execute 10b5-1 plans, ensuring that trades occur at pre-determined intervals. AI tools can also analyse these trades to ensure no conflict with blackout periods or MNPI.

1.4. Strengthening Internal Controls with Technology

Compliance departments should adopt the latest **market surveillance tools** to identify unusual trading activity and flag potential violations of insider trading laws.

- **Integrated Market Surveillance Systems (IMSS)**: Implement an **IMSS** to monitor the trades of company insiders, including **real-time tracking** of stock movements and identifying suspicious patterns. Advanced **AI-based algorithms** can detect outliers in trade volume, timing, and frequency that correlate with MNPI.

Action Step:

- **AI-Driven Insider Monitoring**: Set up **machine learning algorithms** to analyse trading patterns automatically and flag any trading activity that coincides with MNPI disclosures or board-level decisions.

2. Best Practices for Corporate Insiders and Compliance Officers

2.1. Blackout Period Enforcement

Strict adherence to **blackout periods** during **earnings releases**, **merger announcements**, or other significant corporate events is critical.

- **Digital Blackout Alerts**: Use **automated alert systems** that notify corporate insiders when blackout periods start and end. These alerts should be tied into company calendars and trading systems, preventing trades from being executed during these periods.

Action Step:

- **Customizable Blackout Period Alerts**: Compliance officers should implement customizable software that sends out blackout alerts via email and internal messaging systems to all affected employees and key stakeholders.

2.2. Corporate Trading Policies and Internal Audits

Companies should regularly review and update their **insider trading policies** to reflect changes in the law and ensure that employees understand their obligations.

- **Internal Compliance Audits**: Conduct annual internal audits of insider trading practices to ensure adherence to policies. These audits should be independent and overseen by the legal department or an external auditor. Include random sampling of insider trades to verify compliance with pre-clearance and blackout policies.

Action Step:

- **Insider Trading Compliance Dashboard**: Create a compliance dashboard for executives that tracks all trades in real-time, highlights any deviations from policy, and allows for rapid intervention when violations are detected.

3. How Retail Investors Can Protect Themselves from Insider Trading Risks

3.1. Avoiding Suspicious Tips and Stock Advice

Retail investors should avoid acting on suspicious **stock tips** or **inside information** they may receive through acquaintances or brokers. The risks of trading on such information, even unknowingly, include financial loss and potential legal repercussions.

- **Independent Research**: Retail investors should rely on **publicly available information** and do their own research rather than following "hot stock tips." Use credible resources such as **SEC filings, company**

reports, and **market analysis tools** to make informed investment decisions.

Action Step:

- **Investment Education Platforms**: Enroll in online investment education platforms that provide comprehensive tools to analyse stocks based on **fundamentals**, rather than relying on rumours or market sentiment.

3.2. Diversifying Portfolios to Mitigate Risk

Diversification is an essential strategy for protecting against potential losses related to **market manipulation** or insider trading by corporate insiders.

- **Use of ETFs and Index Funds**: Retail investors can reduce their exposure to insider trading risks by investing in **Exchange-Traded Funds (ETFs)** or **Index Funds**, which inherently provide diversification and lower the impact of stock price manipulation in a single company.

Action Step:

- **Portfolio Analysis Tools**: Leverage portfolio analysis tools that allow retail investors to assess their exposure to particular industries or companies and adjust accordingly to maintain a diversified portfolio.

3.3. Leveraging Technology for Market Surveillance

Retail investors can benefit from using technology that aggregates **real-time market data, news sentiment**, and **stock performance analysis** to help spot unusual trading behaviour.

- **Fintech Solutions**: Use fintech platforms like **Robinhood, Wealthfront,** or **E*TRADE**, which offer real-time market updates and customizable alerts on stock movements. Many of these platforms now offer **AI-driven alerts** for detecting sudden price changes or volume spikes.

Action Step:

- **Real-Time Trade Alerts**: Set up real-time trade alerts that notify investors when there are unusual changes in **price, volume,** or **sentiment analysis**. These systems can help retail investors react quickly to avoid market manipulation risks.

4. Role of Whistleblowers in Insider Trading Detection: A Practical Framework

4.1. Establishing Anonymous Whistleblower Programs

Whistleblowers are key to uncovering insider trading within organizations, and companies should establish **anonymous reporting systems** to facilitate this. Providing a secure, confidential environment for whistleblowers encourages early reporting of any unethical activities.

- **Whistleblower Protection Systems**: Implement anonymous hotlines or third-party reporting platforms where employees can report insider trading violations without fear of retaliation.

Action Step:

- **Third-Party Whistleblower Platforms**: Adopt third-party platforms like **Navex Global** or **EthicsPoint**, which allow employees to report suspicious activities while ensuring complete anonymity.

4.2. Incentives and Legal Protections for Whistleblowers

Both **SEBI** and **SEC** offer **financial rewards** to whistleblowers who provide actionable information that leads to successful insider trading enforcement. Companies must also ensure that they comply with **whistleblower protection laws** to avoid retaliation claims.

- **Compliance with Whistleblower Laws**: Ensure that internal policies are aligned with the legal protections offered under **SEBI's Informant Reward Scheme** or **SEC's Whistleblower Program**, including non-retaliation clauses.

Action Step:

- **Whistleblower Policy Awareness Campaigns**: Conduct internal awareness campaigns to inform employees about the company's whistleblower protections, financial incentives available under regulatory programs, and how to report suspicious activity.

4.3. Use of AI for Whistleblower Protection

AI-driven platforms can help analyse whistleblower reports, prioritize them based on risk factors, and expedite investigation processes.

- **Automated Whistleblower Case Management**: Use AI-powered case management software to track whistleblower reports and escalate high-priority cases directly to compliance officers. AI tools can also ensure that whistleblower information is stored securely, reducing the risk of leaks or retaliation.

Action Step:

- **AI-Enhanced Whistleblower Detection**: Leverage AI tools like **Clue** or **Workiva** to analyse reported issues, automatically prioritize cases, and provide recommendations for further investigation based on the severity of the allegations.

Conclusion: Building a Compliance-First Culture

Creating a **culture of compliance** is critical to avoiding the legal and financial risks of insider trading. Professionals, retail investors, and companies must actively engage with evolving **regulations** and **technological advancements** to ensure that they are aligned with best practices for detecting and preventing insider trading violations. By adopting robust internal controls, leveraging cutting-edge technologies, and fostering **transparent reporting mechanisms**, market participants can stay compliant and contribute to **market integrity**.

This practical framework offers actionable steps that companies, compliance officers, professionals, and investors can take to reduce the risks associated with insider trading. From **pre-clearance systems** to **automated whistleblower platforms**, these guidelines integrate data-driven solutions and **global regulatory standards** to ensure compliance and foster trust in financial markets.

Chapter 17

Corporate Governance and Insider Trading

Effective corporate governance serves as the first line of defense against insider trading. It establishes a framework of accountability, transparency, and ethical oversight, ensuring that insiders with access to MNPI adhere to both legal and ethical standards.

The Role of the Board in Mitigating Insider Trading

A well-structured board of directors is crucial in enforcing corporate governance policies that prevent insider trading. Independent board members, those who do not have a vested financial interest in the company, are particularly effective at monitoring insider activity. By separating decision-making from those who stand to gain financially, independent directors ensure a level of objectivity and ethical rigor in corporate governance.

Research conducted by PwC found that companies with active and independent boards reported 40% fewer insider trading violations. This is largely due to the board's oversight in approving trading plans, monitoring corporate disclosures, and implementing blackout periods—times when insiders are prohibited from trading shares due to pending material events

The Role of Audit Committees and Internal Controls

Corporate governance is strengthened through the work of audit committees, which oversee financial disclosures and ensure that internal controls are in place to detect unethical behaviour. The audit committee, composed of independent directors, plays a significant role in monitoring insider trading by reviewing financial statements for any inconsistencies that could signal potential fraud or MNPI leakage.

The Role of External Auditors

External auditors act as an additional layer of defense against insider trading by conducting independent reviews of the company's financial health and ensuring the accuracy of its financial disclosures. The presence of external auditors reduces the likelihood of fraudulent activity and forces insiders to act within the boundaries of legal and financial propriety.

Case Study: Satyam Computers

The Satyam Computers scandal in India highlighted the critical role of corporate governance in preventing insider trading. Weak internal controls allowed the company's leadership to manipulate financial statements, leading to insider trading by top executives. A stronger board and audit committee could have detected these irregularities earlier, preventing the large-scale fraud that ultimately led to the company's collapse.

Chapter 18

Insider Trading in Emerging Markets

Emerging markets present a unique challenge for regulators seeking to enforce insider trading laws. While countries like India, Brazil, and China have established regulatory frameworks, enforcement remains inconsistent, and information asymmetry often creates opportunities for insider trading.

Regulatory Challenges in Emerging Markets

The effectiveness of insider trading regulations in emerging markets is hampered by several factors, including limited regulatory resources, weaker legal frameworks, and political interference. For example, in China, while the Securities Law of 2005 explicitly criminalizes insider trading, the number of prosecutions remains low compared to developed markets. Between 2005 and 2015, China saw only 98 insider trading prosecutions, a fraction of the cases seen in the U.S. during the same period.

Case Study: The Petrobras Scandal

In Brazil, the Petrobras scandal became one of the largest corruption and insider trading cases in **Latin America**. Executives at Petrobras were found to have used MNPI to trade stocks ahead of corporate announcements, generating millions in illegal profits. Despite Operation Car Wash leading to numerous convictions, regulatory enforcement of insider trading laws in Brazil remains fragmented, with many insider trading cases going unpunished.

Improvements in Regulatory Enforcement

In recent years, emerging markets like India have made strides in improving regulatory enforcement. The **Securities and Exchange Board of India (SEBI)** has implemented real-time market surveillance systems like **Integrated Market Surveillance System (IMSS),** which tracks unusual trading patterns in real-time. Since the introduction of these systems, India has seen a marked increase in insider trading prosecutions, with over 350 cases prosecuted since 2015.

Chapter 19

Insider Trading and Corporate Social Responsibility (CSR)

Insider trading goes against the core principles of **Corporate Social Responsibility (CSR)**, which emphasize transparency, fairness, and ethical behaviour in business. Companies with robust CSR frameworks are not only seen as more trustworthy by investors but also less likely to engage in unethical trading practices.

How Insider Trading Violates CSR Principles

Insider trading undermines the trust that stakeholders—shareholders, employees, customers, and the broader public—place in a company. A company that permits or overlooks insider trading sends a clear signal that it prioritizes profit over ethical behaviour, damaging its reputation and undermining the social contract it holds with the community.

Integrating CSR into Insider Trading Prevention

Companies that integrate ethical training programs into their CSR initiatives often report fewer violations. For example, companies like **Nike and Patagonia** have implemented extensive employee training programs that include sessions on ethical trading practices, ensuring employees are well-versed in the legal and ethical boundaries regarding the use of confidential information.

Case Study: Ben & Jerry's

Ben & Jerry's is a leading example of a company that has built ethical behaviour into its corporate DNA. The company has a zero-tolerance policy on insider trading and regularly educates employees on the consequences of unethical behaviour. This proactive approach has allowed Ben & Jerry's to build a strong ethical brand that resonates with socially conscious investors.

Chapter 20

Technology and Insider Trading
The Role of Fintech

Technology is playing a dual role in the world of insider trading: on one hand, it provides new tools for insiders to manipulate the markets, but on the other, it offers regulators unprecedented capabilities to detect and prosecute illegal trading activities.

AI-Driven Surveillance in Insider Trading

Regulators are increasingly using artificial intelligence (AI) to detect insider trading. The **Securities and Exchange Commission (SEC) utilizes AI algorithms** to monitor **1.5 billion trades daily**. These algorithms use pattern recognition to flag abnormal trading volumes and price movements that suggest insider trading activity.

In 2020, AI technology was instrumental in detecting suspicious trades ahead of Elon Musk's tweets that significantly impacted Tesla's stock price. The SEC flagged these trades in real-time, raising concerns about potential market manipulation via social media.

The Role of Blockchain in Enhancing Transparency

Blockchain technology offers a new level of transparency in trading by providing an immutable ledger of transactions. Smart contracts on blockchain platforms can automate and monitor stock trades, ensuring that insider trading violations are flagged immediately. A 2020 Deloitte report predicted that blockchain could reduce insider trading by 45% by creating transparent and auditable trading environments.

Chapter 21

Insider Trading Laws, Regulations, and Penalties Across Different Countries

Insider trading laws vary significantly across the globe, depending on the regulatory frameworks of each country. While most major economies criminalize insider trading, some regions still operate without formal regulations or enforcement mechanisms. Below is a detailed country-wise analysis of insider trading laws, key regulations, penalties, and notable landmark cases that have shaped enforcement.

1. India

Regulatory Body: Securities and Exchange Board of India (SEBI)

Key Legislation: SEBI (Prohibition of Insider Trading) Regulations, 2015

Overview of Laws

In India, insider trading is governed by the **SEBI (Prohibition of Insider Trading) Regulations, 2015**, which prohibits insiders from trading securities while in possession of

unpublished price-sensitive information (UPSI). Insiders are defined as anyone with access to MNPI due to their professional position within the company, such as directors, officers, employees, auditors, or significant shareholders.

Penalties

- **Monetary Fines:** SEBI can impose fines of up to ₹25 crore or three times the profits gained or losses avoided, whichever is higher.

- **Imprisonment:** Violators can face imprisonment for a term of up to 10 years.

- **Bans:** SEBI can ban individuals or companies from participating in securities markets, including preventing them from holding director positions.

Landmark Case: SEBI vs. Rakesh Agrawal

Summary: Rakesh Agrawal, the managing director of **DSQ Software**, was convicted of insider trading after trading on confidential information about an acquisition. SEBI's investigation uncovered that Agrawal used MNPI to profit from stock price changes related to the acquisition. This case was one of the first significant insider trading prosecutions in India and set a precedent for SEBI's enforcement authority.

2. United States

Regulatory Body: Securities and Exchange Commission (SEC)
Key Legislation: Securities Exchange Act of 1934, Rule 10b-5

Overview of Laws

In the U.S., insider trading laws are primarily governed by the **Securities Exchange Act of 1934** under **Section 10(b)** and **Rule 10b-5**, which prohibit the use of **material non-public information (MNPI)** in buying or selling securities. The SEC enforces these laws with the help of the **Department of Justice (DOJ)** in criminal cases. Rule 10b-5 prohibits fraudulent activities and manipulative practices in the buying or selling of securities.

Penalties

- **Monetary Fines**: Individuals may be fined up to **$5 million**, and companies can face fines of up to **$25 million**.

- **Imprisonment**: Criminal convictions can result in up to **20 years of imprisonment** for individuals found guilty of insider trading.

- **Disgorgement**: Civil penalties include **disgorgement** of profits, where violators must return all illegally obtained profits, and may pay fines of up to **three times the profit gained** or **loss avoided**.

Landmark Case: U.S. vs. Rajat Gupta

Summary: Rajat Gupta, a former board member of **Goldman Sachs**, was convicted of insider trading for passing MNPI to **Raj Rajaratnam**, founder of Galleon Group. The case was notable for its use of **wiretap evidence** to prove Gupta's involvement. Gupta was sentenced to **two years in prison** and fined **$5 million**. This case highlighted the use of wiretaps in insider trading prosecutions and increased scrutiny on corporate executives.

Landmark Case: U.S. vs. Martha Stewart

Summary: The **Martha Stewart** case involved the sale of **ImClone Systems** stock based on insider information about a negative FDA decision. While Stewart was not charged with insider trading, she was convicted of obstruction of justice and making false statements. Stewart was sentenced to **five months in prison**, and the case became a symbol of celebrity involvement in white-collar crime.

3. United Kingdom

Regulatory Body: Financial Conduct Authority (FCA)
Key Legislation: Market Abuse Regulation (MAR), Criminal Justice Act 1993

Overview of Laws

In the U.K., insider trading falls under the scope of **Market Abuse Regulation (MAR)**, which aims to prevent **market manipulation** and insider trading. Additionally, the **Criminal Justice Act of 1993** specifically criminalizes insider dealing, making it illegal to trade based on MNPI or to disclose such information to others.

Penalties

- **Imprisonment**: Convicted individuals can face up to **7 years in prison**.
- **Monetary Fines**: There is no limit to the fines that can be imposed, making them potentially severe depending on the case.

- **Director Bans**: The FCA can disqualify individuals from holding director positions in public companies.

Landmark Case: FCA vs. Martyn Dodgson

Summary: In 2016, **Martyn Dodgson**, a former director at **Deutsche Bank**, was convicted of insider trading after sharing confidential information about mergers with **James Sanders**, a stock trader. Dodgson was sentenced to **4.5 years in prison**, one of the longest sentences for insider trading in the U.K. The FCA's use of forensic evidence, including trade analysis and communication records, was instrumental in securing this conviction.

4. Australia

Regulatory Body: Australian Securities and Investments Commission (ASIC)

Key Legislation: Corporations Act 2001

Overview of Laws

Insider trading in Australia is regulated under the **Corporations Act 2001**, which prohibits any person from trading in shares or securities if they possess **price-sensitive information** that is not publicly available. The law applies to company directors, officers, employees, and any other individuals who may have MNPI.

Penalties

- **Imprisonment:** Violators can face up to 10 years in prison.

- **Monetary Fines:** Individuals may be fined up to AUD 1 million or three times the profit gained, whichever is greater.

- **Civil Penalties:** ASIC can also pursue civil cases, where fines may exceed AUD 1 million, depending on the severity of the case.

Landmark Case: ASIC vs. Trevor Flugge

Summary: Trevor Flugge, the former chairman of **AWB Ltd**, was convicted of insider trading after he sold shares before a damning report into AWB's involvement in a scandal with the **United Nations' Oil-for-Food** program was released. Flugge was fined and disqualified from managing corporations for five years. The case was a turning point for ASIC's enforcement of insider trading laws.

5. Japan

Regulatory Body: Financial Services Agency (FSA)
Key Legislation: Financial Instruments and Exchange Act

Overview of Laws

Japan's **Financial Instruments and Exchange Act** governs insider trading, prohibiting individuals with MNPI from trading or tipping others to trade in securities. The FSA enforces these laws and collaborates with the **Tokyo Stock Exchange (TSE)** to detect and investigate violations.

Penalties

- **Monetary Fines**: Individuals can be fined up to **JPY 10 million**, while corporations can face fines of up to **JPY 700 million**.

- **Imprisonment**: The maximum prison sentence for individuals involved in insider trading is **5 years**.

Landmark Case: Olympus Scandal

Summary: The **Olympus Corporation** scandal involved a series of financial misstatements and insider trading violations. Key executives engaged in cover-ups and trades based on MNPI related to the company's financial health. Several top executives were arrested and convicted, sparking reforms in corporate governance and transparency in Japan.

6. Germany

Regulatory Body: Federal Financial Supervisory Authority (BaFin)

Key Legislation: Securities Trading Act (WpHG)

Overview of Laws

In Germany, insider trading is regulated under the **Securities Trading Act (WpHG)**, which aligns with the **European Union's Market Abuse Regulation (MAR)**. The law prohibits trading based on inside information and the unauthorized disclosure of such information.

Penalties

- **Imprisonment**: Convicted individuals can face up to **5 years in prison**.
- **Fines**: Insider trading can result in fines of up to **€5 million**, depending on the severity of the violation.
- **Civil Penalties**: BaFin can impose further financial penalties on corporations involved in insider trading activities.

Landmark Case: Deutsche Börse Insider Trading Scandal

Summary: In 2018, the CEO of **Deutsche Börse**, **Carsten Kengeter**, was investigated for insider trading after purchasing shares shortly before announcing merger talks with the London Stock Exchange. While Kengeter denied any wrongdoing, the investigation led to a significant fine and the restructuring of corporate governance at Deutsche Börse.

7. Canada

Regulatory Body: Ontario Securities Commission (OSC)

Key Legislation: Securities Act (Ontario)

Overview of Laws

Canada's insider trading regulations are governed by provincial securities laws, with the **Ontario Securities Commission (OSC)** being the most influential. The **Securities Act (Ontario)** prohibits trading on MNPI and imposes significant penalties for violations.

Penalties

- **Imprisonment:** Offenders can face up to five years in prison.
- **Fines:** The OSC can impose fines of up to CAD 5 million, along with disgorgement of profits.
- **Trading Bans:** Violators can be banned from serving as directors or officers of publicly traded companies.

Landmark Case: OSC vs. Donald Inkster

Summary: **Donald Inkster**, a former VP of **BioSyntech**, was convicted of insider trading after selling shares based on non-public information about a failed clinical trial. Inkster was fined and sentenced to probation, and the case led to stricter enforcement of insider trading laws in the biotech sector in Canada.

8. Countries Where Insider Trading Is Not Explicitly Illegal

Although insider trading is widely criminalized in most countries, some jurisdictions still lack comprehensive insider trading regulations or enforcement mechanisms. **North Korea** and **some small jurisdictions** with limited financial market activity have no explicit laws banning insider trading. Additionally, in certain emerging markets, insider trading laws are either weakly enforced or still developing, leading to a **lack of prosecutions** and **low regulatory oversight**.

Conclusion

Insider trading is a serious offense across most developed economies, with penalties ranging from significant fines to long-term imprisonment. Regulatory bodies such as **SEBI**, **SEC**, and **FCA** have developed sophisticated surveillance systems to detect and prosecute insider trading activities. However, enforcement still varies globally, with some jurisdictions having more stringent regulations and active prosecutions, while others lag behind. This global regulatory framework continues to evolve, as emerging technologies like **AI** and **blockchain** offer new ways to monitor and prevent insider trading.

Chapter 22

Cross-Border Insider Trading: International Cooperation and Legal Challenges

Introduction

Insider trading is no longer confined to national borders; it has become a global issue that affects financial markets across countries. With the rise of multinational corporations, global stock exchanges, and cross-border investment portfolios, insider trading schemes often span multiple jurisdictions, creating **"significant legal challenges"** for regulators and enforcement agencies.

Cross-border insider trading presents intricate challenges, from navigating legal hurdles to ensuring international cooperation for effective enforcement. Understanding the complexities of extradition and jurisdictional enforcement is crucial, as these issues often hinder the prosecution of financial crimes that span multiple countries. Examining key landmark cases in cross-border insider trading offers valuable insights into the ever-evolving landscape of international financial crime. These cases underscore the increasing need for robust global regulatory collaboration to maintain market integrity and combat illicit activities on a global scale.

1. The Complex Nature of Cross-Border Insider Trading

The globalization of financial markets has made it easier for insiders to exploit information across national borders. As companies expand internationally, their securities are often traded on multiple stock exchanges, creating opportunities for insiders to engage in cross-border insider trading. This complexity is further amplified when trades are executed through offshore accounts, foreign subsidiaries, or intermediaries in different countries.

In cross-border cases, the flow of information and execution of trades may occur in different jurisdictions. For instance, an executive in London may gain **Material Non-Public Information (MNPI)** about a merger involving a company listed on the **New York Stock Exchange (NYSE)**. The executive may then trade on that information in a third country, such as Switzerland, where their account is based. This multi-jurisdictional nature complicates enforcement, as regulators must collaborate across borders to investigate, gather evidence, and prosecute.

2. Jurisdictional Conflicts and Legal Challenges

One of the primary hurdles in prosecuting cross-border insider trading is the issue of jurisdiction. Each country has its own regulatory framework, legal definitions, and penalties for insider trading, and these can vary widely. The differences in insider trading laws, evidence collection standards, and court procedures can create jurisdictional conflicts, making it difficult for regulators to coordinate enforcement efforts.

2.1. Differing Definitions and Laws

- **Material Non-Public Information (MNPI):** The definition of what constitutes MNPI varies across countries. While most jurisdictions agree that MNPI includes confidential information that can affect a company's stock price, the scope of what qualifies as **"material"** can differ. For instance, in the United States, MNPI encompasses any information that a reasonable investor would consider important, whereas in Europe, the definition under the **Market Abuse Regulation (MAR)** is more narrowly interpreted.

- **Criminal vs. Civil Offenses:** Some countries treat insider trading primarily as a civil offense, punishable by fines and market bans (**e.g., Germany and Japan**), while others, like the United States and India, view insider trading as a criminal offense, with penalties that include imprisonment.

- **Case Study:** Raj Rajaratnam (U.S. and Europe) The case of Raj Rajaratnam, founder of the Galleon Group, involved insider trading activities in both the U.S. and Europe. Rajaratnam obtained confidential information about U.S. companies with European operations. Although the bulk of his prosecution occurred in the U.S., European regulators were involved due to the multinational nature of the companies traded. Differences in legal interpretations between the SEC and European regulators delayed parts of the investigation, highlighting jurisdictional conflicts.

2.2. Legal Challenges in Evidence Gathering

Gathering evidence in cross-border cases can be particularly difficult due to differences in privacy laws, data protection regulations, and securities disclosure requirements. In some jurisdictions, strict privacy laws make it difficult for regulators to obtain trade logs, communication records, and bank statements, which are crucial for building a case against suspected insider traders.

- **Data Protection Laws:** The General Data Protection Regulation (GDPR) in the European Union limits the ability of regulators to access personal data, which can include trading records and communications related to insider trading. This is particularly challenging when information needs to be shared with non-EU regulators such as the SEC or FINRA.

- **Cooperation from Foreign Entities:** Multinational corporations and offshore financial institutions may be reluctant to cooperate with foreign regulators due to concerns about violating local laws or alienating clients. This can result in delays in obtaining crucial documents or accessing financial records located abroad.

3. International Regulatory Cooperation

Given the complex nature of cross-border insider trading, international cooperation is essential for effective enforcement. Regulators around the world have developed multilateral agreements, memoranda of understanding (MOUs), and informal networks to share information, conduct joint investigations, and prosecute offenders.

3.1. International Organization of Securities Commissions (IOSCO)

One of the most important bodies for fostering international cooperation on securities regulation is the International Organization of Securities Commissions (IOSCO). IOSCO is composed of securities regulators from more than 115 countries, including SEBI (India), SEC (U.S.), and FCA (U.K.). It serves as a global forum where regulators can exchange information, set common standards, and facilitate cross-border enforcement.

- **IOSCO's Multilateral Memorandum of Understanding (MMoU):** The MMoU is a legally binding agreement that enables IOSCO member countries to share non-public information, conduct joint investigations, and assist in enforcing securities laws across borders. The MMoU has been instrumental in several high-profile insider trading cases by enabling seamless communication between regulators in different jurisdictions.

3.2. Bilateral Agreements

In addition to multilateral cooperation through IOSCO, many countries have entered into bilateral agreements to facilitate cross-border securities enforcement. For example, the SEC has bilateral MOUs with regulators in over 25 countries, allowing for more targeted information sharing and coordinated investigations.

- **Case Study:** SEC and FSA (U.K.) Cooperation in the Chris Kao Case The SEC and the U.K.'s Financial Services Authority (FSA) collaborated on the insider trading case involving Chris Kao, a London-based trader. Kao traded on MNPI related to a U.S.-listed company, using accounts based in the U.K. The SEC's MOU with the FSA allowed for the exchange of trading records and communications, leading to Kao's conviction.

3.3. Interpol and Cross-Border Investigations

In some cases, Interpol is involved in cross-border financial crime investigations, including insider trading. Interpol's Financial Crimes Unit assists national regulators in tracking suspects, freezing assets, and facilitating extradition when necessary.

4. Challenges in Cross-Border Enforcement

Despite these efforts, significant challenges remain in enforcing insider trading laws across borders. These include:

4.1. The Challenge of Extradition

Extraditing individuals accused of insider trading can be a lengthy and complex process. Many countries are reluctant to extradite their citizens for financial crimes, especially if insider trading is considered a minor offense in that jurisdiction. Furthermore, differences in extradition treaties and legal definitions of insider trading can complicate matters.

- **Case Study:** Samir Barai (U.S. and India) Samir Barai, a hedge fund manager implicated in an insider trading scandal in the U.S., fled to India before he could be arrested. The U.S. sought Barai's extradition, but legal challenges in India delayed the process for years. The lack of a clear extradition agreement for financial crimes between the two countries further complicated the matter.

4.2. Variations in Penalties and Enforcement Intensity

Even when insider trading is proven, the penalties can vary widely depending on the jurisdiction. For example, while the U.S. imposes severe prison sentences (up to 20 years) and heavy fines, many European countries impose much lighter penalties. This discrepancy can create a regulatory arbitrage, where traders exploit less stringent legal environments to engage in illegal activity.

- **Example: In Germany,** insider trading is often treated as a civil offense, with penalties primarily consisting of fines. This stands in stark contrast to the criminal penalties imposed in the U.S., where insider trading convictions frequently result in imprisonment.

4.3. Length of Investigations

Cross-border investigations can be protracted due to the time it takes to gather and authenticate evidence from multiple jurisdictions. Regulators must navigate various legal systems, deal with language barriers, and comply with different standards of proof. These delays can jeopardize the timeliness of prosecution, with insider traders often taking advantage of the time lag to relocate assets or evade capture.

5. Cross-Border Insider Trading Cases

Several landmark cross-border insider trading cases demonstrate both the complexity and the success of international cooperation. These cases illustrate the evolving nature of global financial crime and the concerted efforts of regulators worldwide to bring wrongdoers to justice.

UBS and Swiss Insider Trading Case

A significant insider trading investigation occurred involving UBS, where Swiss regulators worked with their counterparts in the U.S. and U.K. to uncover a scheme that used confidential information about mergers to make profitable trades. The complexity of Swiss banking secrecy laws delayed the investigation, but international cooperation eventually led to significant fines for the traders involved.

Conclusion

Cross-border insider trading presents a formidable challenge to regulators worldwide. The globalization of financial markets has created opportunities for sophisticated insider trading schemes that span multiple countries, often exploiting differences in legal frameworks and enforcement intensities. However, through international cooperation, bilateral agreements, and organizations like IOSCO, regulators have made significant strides in detecting and prosecuting cross-border insider trading cases.

Chapter 23

Insider Trading in the Digital Era: Cryptocurrency and NFTs

Introduction

The rise of digital assets, particularly cryptocurrencies and non-fungible tokens (NFTs), has revolutionized financial markets by creating decentralized, borderless trading environments. While these innovations have enabled new opportunities for investment, they have also introduced new forms of market manipulation—including insider trading. Unlike traditional stock markets, where insider trading laws are well-established and rigorously enforced, the world of cryptocurrencies and NFTs remains largely unregulated, presenting challenges for regulatory bodies and investors alike.

In this chapter, we will explore how insider trading occurs in the crypto world, examine the lack of comprehensive regulation, and analyse notable cases that have shaped the debate on how digital assets should be regulated. We will also look toward the future of regulation, as global bodies like the Securities and Exchange Commission (SEC) and Financial

Conduct Authority (FCA) consider integrating cryptocurrencies and NFTs into traditional insider trading frameworks.

How Insider Trading Occurs in the Crypto World

Insider trading in traditional stock markets involves the use of material non-public information (MNPI) by insiders to make profitable trades. In the cryptocurrency world, this practice takes on new dimensions due to the decentralized nature of these assets, the lack of centralized exchanges, and the speed at which information spreads. Insiders in the cryptocurrency space often leverage their privileged access to MNPI to manipulate the market, with Initial Coin Offerings (ICOs) and technological advancements being prime opportunities for illegal profit-making.

Initial Coin Offerings (ICOs) and Insider Trading

ICOs, the cryptocurrency equivalent of an Initial Public Offering (IPO), are one of the most common opportunities for insider trading in the digital space. In an ICO, a company or organization raises funds by issuing new digital tokens to investors, often before these tokens are listed on public exchanges. Insiders—such as company executives, developers, or early investors—often have access to non-public information about the timing and success of the ICO.

Pre-ICO Announcements: Insiders with advance knowledge of an upcoming ICO or pre-sale events can buy tokens before they become publicly available, reaping substantial profits once the tokens are listed and the price increases. This practice mirrors traditional insider trading, where early access to information about a company's financial performance or upcoming merger drives illicit trades.

Pump-and-Dump Schemes: In the cryptocurrency space, pump-and-dump schemes are rampant. Here, insiders coordinate to artificially inflate the price of a new token (the "pump") by creating hype around the ICO or project, often using false or exaggerated information. Once the price skyrockets, insiders sell their holdings (the "dump"), leaving unsuspecting retail investors with depreciated assets.

Example: In 2017, the Centra Tech ICO—promoted by high-profile celebrities—was revealed to be a scam, and its founders were charged with securities fraud and insider trading. The insiders sold their tokens after hyping the project, leaving investors with worthless tokens.

Chapter 24

Insider Trading and Technological Developments

In the volatile world of cryptocurrencies, technological updates, such as protocol upgrades, network forks, or the implementation of new features, can have a significant impact on token prices. Insiders, particularly developers and engineers, often have advance knowledge of these changes and can exploit this information to trade ahead of the market.

- **Network Forks:** A network fork occurs when a blockchain splits into two separate chains, often resulting in the creation of a new cryptocurrency. Insiders with knowledge of an impending fork, such as the Bitcoin Cash fork in 2017, can position themselves to profit by buying the original token and receiving the forked token upon its release. This practice is akin to trading on MNPI in traditional markets.

- **Security Vulnerabilities:** Cryptocurrencies rely heavily on secure networks to maintain trust in the ecosystem. Insiders who discover security vulnerabilities or impending patches can manipulate the market by short-selling a cryptocurrency before the vulnerability is publicly disclosed.

The Lack of Regulation in Crypto Markets

One of the biggest challenges in combating insider trading in the cryptocurrency and NFT markets is the lack of comprehensive regulatory frameworks. Unlike traditional financial markets, which are heavily regulated by bodies such as the SEC in the U.S. and the FCA in the U.K., the cryptocurrency world operates largely outside the purview of these institutions.

Decentralization and Pseudonymity

Cryptocurrencies were designed to operate in a decentralized manner, meaning there is no central authority, such as a stock exchange or regulatory body, that oversees transactions. While decentralization is one of the main advantages of cryptocurrencies, it also makes it much harder to enforce insider trading laws.

- **Pseudonymity:** Many cryptocurrency transactions are conducted under pseudonymous addresses, making it difficult to trace the identities of the traders involved. Without knowing the identity of the traders, regulators cannot easily determine if someone is trading on MNPI. This has been one of the primary roadblocks to enforcing insider trading laws in the cryptocurrency space.

- **Offshore Exchanges:** Many cryptocurrency exchanges are based in offshore jurisdictions with lax regulatory environments. These exchanges often do not require users to undergo strict KYC (Know Your Customer) procedures, making it easy for insiders to hide their identities and evade detection.

Lack of Clear Legal Definitions

Most jurisdictions do not have clear legal definitions for what constitutes insider trading in the context of digital assets. While the U.S. SEC has begun applying existing securities laws to certain cryptocurrencies, many other countries have yet to establish frameworks that specifically address digital assets.

- **Are Cryptocurrencies Securities?:** A fundamental legal question is whether cryptocurrencies should be classified as securities, commodities, or something else entirely. In 2018, the SEC determined that Bitcoin and Ethereum are not securities, while other digital assets that were sold through ICOs may be considered securities. However, this lack of a unified global standard creates confusion and regulatory gaps.

- **Jurisdictional Issues:** Cryptocurrency transactions often occur across borders, complicating regulatory enforcement. For example, if an insider based in China trades on a U.S.-based exchange using a European account, it becomes unclear which country's regulations, if any, apply.

3. Notable Cases of Insider Trading in Cryptocurrency

Despite the lack of comprehensive regulation, some insider trading cases in the cryptocurrency space have garnered significant attention. These cases highlight the vulnerabilities of the unregulated nature of digital markets and have spurred calls for greater oversight.

3.1. Coinbase Insider Trading Scandal

In 2022, the **U.S. Department of Justice (DOJ)** charged a former Coinbase product manager and two others with insider trading. The Coinbase employees allegedly used non-public information about upcoming cryptocurrency listings to trade and profit. This case marked the first insider trading prosecution involving cryptocurrencies in the U.S. and set a precedent for applying existing securities laws to the crypto market.

- **The Details:** The product manager had access to confidential information about which cryptocurrencies would be listed on Coinbase. Before public announcements, the individuals bought large amounts of these cryptocurrencies, knowing that a listing on a major exchange like Coinbase would lead to a price surge.

- **Legal Ramifications:** The defendants were charged with wire fraud, as cryptocurrency trading was not explicitly covered by traditional insider trading laws. However, this case sparked debate about whether crypto assets should fall under securities laws and led to discussions about modernizing regulations.

3.2. The Ripple (XRP) Case

In December 2020, the SEC filed a lawsuit against Ripple Labs, alleging that the company and its executives engaged in the sale of unregistered securities in the form of XRP tokens. The SEC argued that Ripple's executives profited from their insider knowledge of the company's future plans, selling XRP tokens while withholding crucial information from investors.

- **Significance:** This case is significant because it raises questions about whether XRP should be classified as a security. The lawsuit could set a precedent for how other cryptocurrencies are regulated and whether insider trading laws will apply to these assets in the future.

4. Future Regulations: Integrating Cryptocurrency into Insider Trading Laws

As the cryptocurrency market continues to grow, global regulatory bodies are increasingly focusing on developing clear and enforceable insider trading laws for digital assets. The SEC, FCA, and other national regulators have started integrating cryptocurrencies into existing securities frameworks, but many questions remain about how best to regulate this rapidly evolving market.

4.1. SEC's Approach to Cryptocurrencies

The U.S. SEC has taken an active role in regulating certain cryptocurrencies under existing securities laws. In several high-profile cases, the SEC has classified certain ICOs as unregistered securities offerings, and it has brought enforcement actions against companies and individuals for violating insider trading laws.

- **Regulatory Clarity for Digital Assets:** The SEC has indicated that it will continue to regulate cryptocurrencies that it considers securities, and the 2021 Coinbase insider trading case suggests that the SEC is willing to apply traditional insider trading laws to the crypto space. However, there remains a lack of comprehensive guidance about which cryptocurrencies fall under securities laws and how decentralized exchanges will be regulated.

4.2. FCA's Role in Crypto Regulation

In the U.K., the **Financial Conduct Authority (FCA)** has also begun to regulate digital assets. The FCA has required cryptocurrency companies to register under its **Anti-Money Laundering (AML)** regulations, and it has taken steps to regulate crypto derivatives. However, insider trading laws in the U.K. are not yet fully applicable to cryptocurrency markets.

- **Focus on Investor Protection:** The FCA has emphasized the need to protect investors in the volatile cryptocurrency market. While insider trading in traditional markets is well-regulated under the **Market Abuse Regulation (MAR)**, the FCA is still in the process of determining how insider trading rules will apply to digital assets.

4.3. Global Coordination on Cryptocurrency Regulation

As cryptocurrency trading often crosses international borders, global coordination is essential for effective regulation. Organizations such as the **International Organization of Securities Commissions (IOSCO)** are working to establish common standards for regulating digital assets, including the enforcement of insider trading laws.

- **Challenges of Cross-Border Regulation:** The decentralized nature of cryptocurrencies and the use of offshore exchanges make cross-border enforcement difficult. Countries will need to collaborate on creating extradition agreements, data-sharing protocols, and common regulatory frameworks to prevent insiders from exploiting regulatory gaps.

Conclusion

Insider trading in the digital era is a rapidly evolving issue, with cryptocurrencies and NFTs presenting new challenges for regulators. The decentralized and largely unregulated nature of these markets has created opportunities for insiders to exploit MNPI for profit, while the lack of comprehensive legal frameworks has made enforcement difficult. However, notable cases such as the Coinbase insider trading scandal and the Ripple lawsuit are setting precedents that may shape the future of regulation in this space.

As global regulatory bodies like **the SEC and FCA** continue to explore how best to integrate cryptocurrencies into traditional insider trading laws, it is clear that the regulation of digital assets will become an increasingly important issue in the coming years. Effective regulation will require international cooperation, clear legal definitions, and advanced surveillance technologies to ensure that digital markets operate with the same level of transparency and fairness as traditional financial markets.

Chapter 25

The Role of Whistleblowers in Insider Trading Prosecutions: Legal Protections and Incentives

Introduction

Whistleblowers have become one of the most powerful tools in exposing **insider trading** and other forms of **financial misconduct**. In the context of insider trading, whistleblowers—often insiders themselves—play a pivotal role in providing **material non-public information (MNPI)** to regulators and prosecutors, which can lead to successful investigations and convictions. By reporting unethical or illegal activities, whistleblowers help ensure **market integrity, transparency**, and **fairness** in financial markets.

However, the decision to come forward with sensitive information is often fraught with risks, including **career damage, retaliation**, and **legal ramifications**. To mitigate these risks and encourage individuals to report wrongdoing, many countries have established **legal protections** and **financial incentives** for whistleblowers, particularly in the context of insider trading cases. In this chapter, we will explore the role of whistleblowers in insider trading prosecutions, examine the **legal frameworks** that protect them, analyse **incentive structures** across different jurisdictions, and discuss **notable whistleblower cases** that have shaped the legal landscape.

1. The Role of Whistleblowers in Exposing Insider Trading

In insider trading cases, whistleblowers are often individuals who are **privy to sensitive information** about illicit activities within an organization. These individuals can be **company employees, executives, auditors**, or **third-party contractors** who witness illegal trading activities or have access to MNPI that they believe is being exploited for personal gain. Whistleblowers can provide **evidence** that is otherwise difficult for regulators to uncover, especially in highly secretive and complex financial schemes.

1.1. How Whistleblowers Provide Evidence

Whistleblowers often have access to **internal documents**, **emails**, and **communication logs** that provide critical evidence for regulators such as the **Securities and Exchange Commission (SEC)** or the **Financial Conduct Authority (FCA)**. This evidence can include:

- **Insider communications** that discuss the use of MNPI to profit from stock trades.
- **Financial transactions** or trade logs showing patterns of suspicious trading activity that coincide with major corporate announcements.
- **Internal memos or meeting notes** where executives or key employees discuss impending mergers, acquisitions,

or earnings reports, which are later exploited for personal gain.

- **Whistleblower reports** detailing the steps taken by the insider to conceal the illegal trades or financial gains.

In many cases, whistleblowers provide the **smoking gun** that leads to a deeper investigation and eventual prosecution.

2. Legal Protections for Whistleblowers in Insider Trading Cases

Whistleblowers often face significant **risks** when coming forward to report insider trading activities, including **retaliation, loss of employment**, and **legal consequences** from their own involvement in the misconduct. To encourage individuals to report unethical behaviour and protect them from these risks, many countries have enacted **legal frameworks** designed to shield whistleblowers from retaliation and provide them with **anonymity**.

2.1. U.S. Legal Protections: The Dodd-Frank Act

In the United States, the **Dodd-Frank Wall Street Reform and Consumer Protection Act** of 2010 created robust legal protections for whistleblowers who report insider trading and other securities violations. The act empowers the **SEC's Office of the Whistleblower** to protect individuals who come forward with information about corporate malfeasance.

- **Anti-Retaliation Provisions**: Under **Dodd-Frank**, employers are prohibited from retaliating against employees who report insider trading. If a whistleblower is terminated, demoted, or otherwise retaliated against, they can file a lawsuit and may be awarded **reinstatement, back pay,** and **compensation** for damages.

- **Confidentiality and Anonymity**: Whistleblowers can submit tips anonymously if they are represented by an attorney. This allows individuals to report without fear of being publicly identified, which is crucial in sensitive cases where the whistleblower may face professional or personal retaliation.

2.2. Legal Protections in the European Union: The EU Whistleblower Directive

In the European Union, the **EU Whistleblower Protection Directive**, adopted in 2019, establishes a framework for protecting whistleblowers who report violations of EU law, including insider trading and market abuse.

- **Protection Against Retaliation**: The directive requires all EU member states to enact laws that protect whistleblowers from **dismissal, demotion,** and other forms of retaliation. Whistleblowers who experience retaliation are entitled to seek remedies such as reinstatement and financial compensation.

- **Reporting Channels**: The directive mandates the establishment of secure **internal** and **external reporting channels** to ensure that whistleblowers can report misconduct to regulators without fear of exposure.

- **Cross-Border Whistleblowing**: Given the cross-border nature of many insider trading cases in Europe, the directive also facilitates cooperation between regulators in different EU member states to ensure that whistleblowers are protected across jurisdictions.

2.3. Protections in Other Jurisdictions

Countries like **India, Australia**, and **Canada** have also developed whistleblower protection laws to shield individuals who report insider trading.

- **India**: In India, **SEBI's Prohibition of Insider Trading Regulations, 2015** includes provisions for whistleblowers to report insider trading without facing retaliation. The **Whistleblower Protection Act, 2014** also provides additional safeguards for individuals who report corporate malfeasance.

- **Australia**: The **Corporations Act 2001** offers protection for whistleblowers who report insider trading. Under this law, whistleblowers are entitled to **confidentiality**, and employers are prohibited from taking **adverse actions** against them.

- **Canada**: The **Ontario Securities Commission (OSC)** offers whistleblower protections through its **Whistleblower Program**, which allows whistleblowers to report anonymously and provides anti-retaliation protections.

3. Financial Incentives for Whistleblowers: Global Perspectives

To encourage more whistleblowers to come forward, many countries provide **financial incentives** for individuals who report insider trading and other securities violations. These

monetary rewards are typically based on the **value of the sanctions** imposed as a result of the whistleblower's tip.

3.1. U.S. Whistleblower Rewards Program

The U.S. **SEC's Whistleblower Program**, established under Dodd-Frank, is one of the most successful and well-known whistleblower reward systems in the world. Whistleblowers who provide original information that leads to successful enforcement actions can receive **10% to 30%** of the total monetary sanctions collected by the SEC.

- **Significant Payouts**: Since the inception of the program in 2011, the SEC has awarded over **$1.3 billion** to whistleblowers. In 2020 alone, the SEC paid a record **$114 million** to a single whistleblower whose information led to a successful enforcement action, marking the largest payout in the program's history.

- **Eligibility**: To be eligible for a reward, the whistleblower's information must be **original**, meaning it cannot be publicly available or derived from another source. The information must lead to an enforcement action resulting in monetary sanctions exceeding **$1 million**.

3.2. The U.K.'s Approach to Whistleblower Rewards

Unlike the U.S., the **U.K. Financial Conduct Authority (FCA)** does not currently offer financial rewards for whistleblowers. However, the **FCA** has considered adopting a similar program in the future. Instead, the U.K. focuses on **legal protections** and **anonymity** to encourage whistleblowers to report wrongdoing. There is growing debate within the U.K.

financial community about whether a financial reward system would further incentivize individuals to report insider trading.

3.3. The EU's Debate on Whistleblower Incentives

The **European Union** has taken a more cautious approach to offering financial incentives for whistleblowers. While the EU's **Whistleblower Protection Directive** offers robust legal protections, it does not include provisions for financial rewards. However, some EU member states, such as **Germany** and **France**, have debated whether financial incentives could strengthen insider trading enforcement.

3.4. Emerging Markets and Whistleblower Rewards

In **emerging markets**, such as **India** and **Brazil**, financial incentives for whistleblowers are still in their infancy. However, regulatory bodies in these regions are beginning to recognize the value of whistleblower programs in detecting insider trading and other market abuses.

- **India**: The **SEBI** has recently introduced financial incentives for whistleblowers, with rewards of up to ₹10 **lakh** for information leading to a successful enforcement action. This is part of SEBI's broader effort to enhance market transparency and reduce insider trading in India's growing financial markets.

4. Notable Whistleblower Cases in Insider Trading Prosecutions

Several high-profile insider trading cases have been successfully prosecuted thanks to whistleblowers. These cases demonstrate the crucial role that whistleblowers play in providing regulators with the evidence they need to build a case against **insider traders**.

4.1. The Rajat Gupta Case

One of the most famous insider trading cases involving a whistleblower is the prosecution of **Rajat Gupta**, a former board member of **Goldman Sachs** and **Procter & Gamble**. In 2011, a whistleblower came forward with information that Gupta had tipped off hedge fund manager **Raj Rajaratnam** with inside information about Goldman Sachs' financial performance during the 2008 financial crisis.

- **Outcome**: Gupta was convicted of insider trading and sentenced to **two years in prison**. The whistleblower in this case provided crucial information that helped the SEC and DOJ build their case against Gupta.

4.2. The SAC Capital Case

In the case of **SAC Capital Advisors**, one of the largest insider trading scandals in history, whistleblowers played a critical role in exposing illegal trades made by **Steven A. Cohen's** hedge fund. Multiple employees of SAC came forward with evidence that executives had traded on MNPI related to pharmaceutical companies.

- **Outcome**: SAC Capital was fined **$1.8 billion**, and several employees were convicted of insider trading. Although Cohen himself was not charged, the whistleblower tips were instrumental in securing the massive financial penalties against SAC.

4.3. The Tesla Whistleblower Case

In 2019, a whistleblower at **Tesla** reported that the company had engaged in **securities fraud** and insider trading. The whistleblower, a former employee, alleged that Tesla executives had manipulated the company's stock price by providing false financial information to investors. The whistleblower's information triggered an SEC investigation, and although no charges were filed, the case highlights the potential role whistleblowers can play in exposing insider trading at large companies.

5. The Future of Whistleblower Programs in Insider Trading Cases

As insider trading schemes become more sophisticated, whistleblowers will continue to be a vital resource for regulators in detecting and prosecuting financial misconduct. Moving forward, several trends are likely to shape the role of whistleblowers in insider trading cases:

5.1. Expansion of Whistleblower Protections Globally

Many countries are moving toward adopting **U.S.-style whistleblower protection** laws, offering both legal protections and financial incentives to encourage individuals to report insider trading. Emerging markets, in particular, are recognizing the importance of whistleblower programs in maintaining market integrity.

5.2. Use of Technology to Protect Whistleblowers

Advances in technology, such as **encrypted communication platforms** and **blockchain**, are making it easier for whistleblowers to report misconduct without fear of exposure. These technologies allow whistleblowers to securely share information with regulators while maintaining their anonymity.

5.3. Increased Financial Incentives

As seen with the SEC's successful whistleblower program, financial incentives can significantly increase the number of tips received by regulators. Countries that do not yet offer rewards, such as the U.K. and many EU member states, may begin to adopt similar programs to enhance insider trading enforcement.

Conclusion

Whistleblowers are indispensable in the fight against **insider trading**. By providing regulators with **critical evidence** and **insider knowledge**, they help to uncover complex schemes that would otherwise remain hidden. Legal protections such as those offered by the **Dodd-Frank Act** and the **EU Whistleblower Directive** are essential for ensuring that whistleblowers can report misconduct without fear of retaliation.

Financial incentives further encourage individuals to come forward, as seen in the success of the **SEC's Whistleblower Program**, which has awarded over $1 billion in payouts. As the legal landscape evolves, and as insider trading becomes more sophisticated, whistleblowers will continue to play a crucial role in maintaining market integrity and ensuring that financial markets remain fair and transparent for all participants.

Chapter 26

Conclusion: Insider Trading – The Road to Ethical and Compliant Markets

Insider trading is a violation that transcends national borders, industry sectors, and individual roles, making it a focal point of regulatory scrutiny and corporate governance. As it has been explored in this book, insider trading undermines the fairness of financial markets, distorts price discovery, and erodes investor confidence. To combat these detrimental effects, there is a growing need for a **comprehensive, proactive approach** that integrates stringent regulations, cutting-edge technologies, and a culture of ethical compliance within corporations and financial institutions.

This expanded conclusion will delve into the **key takeaways**, examine the **future trends and developments** in insider trading regulation, and offer final reflections on how ethical practices can restore **market integrity**.

Summary of Key Takeaways

1. Understanding Insider Trading Laws: The Global Perspective

Insider trading laws differ across jurisdictions but share a common goal: **protecting market integrity**. In countries like the U.S., insider trading is prosecuted under **SEC Rule 10b-5**, while in India, SEBI's **Prohibition of Insider Trading Regulations, 2015** lays down the framework for enforcement. Across Europe, the **Market Abuse Regulation (MAR)** plays a similar role.

- **Compliance** is not just about avoiding illegal activity; it's about creating a **level playing field** for all market participants.

- **Material Non-Public Information (MNPI)** is at the heart of insider trading violations. Information that could impact an investor's decision to buy or sell securities must remain confidential until it is disclosed publicly.

Actionable Insights:

- **Professionals** must familiarize themselves with insider trading laws in their jurisdiction and implement best practices for compliance.

- **Corporate insiders** should be well-versed in what constitutes MNPI and must adhere to **trading windows**, **blackout periods**, and **pre-clearance requirements**.

2. Corporate Compliance and Monitoring Mechanisms

Corporate insiders, particularly **executives**, **directors**, and **officers**, are at a high risk of inadvertently violating insider trading laws due to their access to sensitive information. To mitigate this risk, companies need to establish **strong compliance frameworks** that include the following:

- **Trading Plans and Pre-Clearance Procedures**: Rule **10b5-1 plans** allow insiders to execute pre-scheduled trades, ensuring that their trading decisions are not influenced by MNPI.

- **Automated Surveillance Systems**: Tools like **Integrated Market Surveillance Systems (IMSS)** and **Trade Analysis Software (TAS)** can monitor insider trades in real time, flagging any suspicious activity for compliance officers to investigate.

Actionable Insights:

- **Pre-trade clearance systems** should be mandatory for corporate insiders, ensuring compliance with trading restrictions and legal frameworks.

- Companies must invest in **surveillance tools** that can track trading patterns, detect anomalies, and prevent insider trading before it occurs.

3. The Role of Retail Investors in Insider Trading Prevention

Retail investors, though not typically the perpetrators of insider trading, are often its victims. They can protect themselves by being vigilant and conducting independent research.

- **Avoid Suspicious Tips**: Retail investors should be wary of "hot tips" from brokers or acquaintances, as acting on MNPI can expose them to legal risks.

- **Diversification**: A **well-diversified portfolio** helps mitigate the risk of being disproportionately affected by stock manipulation or insider trading scandals.

Actionable Insights:

- Retail investors should use **financial tools** like **AI-driven trading platforms** and **real-time market alerts** to detect unusual activity and avoid being caught up in insider trading schemes.

- **Education** is key—investors must continuously update their knowledge of market regulations and be aware of the risks posed by insider trading.

4. Forensic Evidence and Cross-Border Enforcement

One of the most critical aspects of prosecuting insider trading cases is the ability to gather and interpret **forensic evidence**. This includes:

- **Digital Forensics**: Techniques such as **wiretaps, email audits**, and **data recovery** are essential for building insider trading cases.

- **Global Cooperation**: Many insider trading cases involve cross-border trades, making **international regulatory cooperation** vital for enforcing insider trading laws.

Actionable Insights:
- Forensic evidence must be meticulously gathered and analysed using advanced technology, including **AI algorithms** that can detect unusual market behaviour in real-time.
- Regulatory bodies like **SEBI**, the **SEC**, and the **FCA** must continue to foster **cross-border collaborations** to tackle global insider trading networks.

5. Whistleblowers as Catalysts for Market Integrity

Whistleblowers have become an essential component in detecting and prosecuting insider trading. Regulatory bodies such as the **SEC** and **SEBI** have created robust whistleblower programs that offer **financial incentives** and **legal protections**.

- **Financial Rewards**: In the U.S., whistleblowers can receive between **10% and 30%** of the sanctions collected from a successful insider trading prosecution.
- **Legal Protections**: Whistleblowers are protected from retaliation, allowing them to report violations anonymously without fear of losing their jobs or facing harassment.

Actionable Insights:
- Companies must create **internal whistleblower mechanisms** that are both **secure** and **transparent**, encouraging employees to report unethical behaviour without fear.
- Regulatory bodies need to continually update and **expand their whistleblower protections**, ensuring whistleblowers feel safe and supported.

The Future of Insider Trading Regulations: Trends and Developments

The future of insider trading regulations is likely to be shaped by technological advancements, regulatory harmonization, and an increased focus on **corporate governance**. Below are some of the key trends and developments to expect:

1. Advancements in Surveillance Technology

The rise of **AI, machine learning**, and **blockchain** will play a critical role in the future of insider trading prevention and detection.

- **AI-Driven Surveillance**: The integration of **AI algorithms** into **market surveillance** systems will enable regulators to detect insider trading patterns more quickly and accurately. These algorithms can analyse vast amounts of data, flagging suspicious trades in real-time and even predicting future violations based on historical patterns.

- **Blockchain for Market Transparency**: The implementation of **blockchain technology** in stock exchanges and trading platforms will create **immutable ledgers** that record every transaction. This will make it easier for regulators to track trades and identify insider trading schemes by providing a **permanent, auditable trail** of every security transaction.

Impact:

- Expect faster, more precise **real-time surveillance** systems powered by AI, making insider trading more difficult to conceal. Blockchain's transparency will further minimize opportunities for fraudulent trades.

2. Global Harmonization of Insider Trading Laws

As financial markets continue to globalize, insider trading schemes increasingly span multiple jurisdictions. Regulators will work toward **global harmonization** of insider trading laws, ensuring consistent enforcement across countries.

- **International Cooperation**: Cross-border cooperation among regulators, such as through **IOSCO's Multilateral Memorandum of Understanding (MMoU)**, will facilitate the sharing of data and evidence, making it easier to prosecute insider trading offenses that involve foreign markets.

- **Unified Legal Frameworks**: Regulatory bodies will likely seek to establish **common standards** for defining MNPI, penalties for violations, and compliance requirements, making it more difficult for insiders to exploit legal loopholes in different jurisdictions.

Impact:

- **Global enforcement** efforts will improve, reducing the chances of insider traders escaping prosecution by moving their activities across borders.

3. Enhanced Corporate Governance and Accountability

Increased scrutiny will be placed on corporate governance practices to ensure that **insider trading policies** are not only enforced but also ingrained in the company's culture.

- **Executive Accountability**: Corporate boards and executives will face heightened expectations around **transparency** and **compliance**. New regulations could hold executives directly accountable for failing to implement adequate insider trading controls within their organizations.

Impact:

- Corporations will need to adopt more rigorous **governance structures** and enforce compliance from the top down, reducing the incidence of insider trading.

4. Stricter Penalties and Expanded Legal Provisions

As the crackdown on insider trading intensifies, **penalties** for violations will likely increase, with extended prison terms, steeper fines, and broader enforcement of **civil liabilities**. The regulatory focus will also expand to cover new areas of concern, such as **insider trading in digital assets** like **cryptocurrencies**.

- **Digital Asset Regulation**: As cryptocurrencies become more integrated into the global financial system, regulators will focus on **monitoring insider trading** in the digital asset market. Expect enhanced scrutiny around **initial coin offerings (ICOs)** and the use of **decentralized exchanges** for insider trading.

Impact:

- **Harsh penalties** for insider trading will serve as a greater deterrent, and the legal framework will broaden to cover **emerging financial markets** such as cryptocurrency.

Final Thoughts on Market Integrity and Ethical Trading Practices

In a world where **information** drives markets, the temptation to exploit non-public information is significant. However, **market integrity** depends on the ability of all participants to operate on a level playing field, where **transparency**, **fairness**, and **ethical behaviour** are upheld. Insider trading erodes trust, not only between individual market participants but also in the broader economic system.

1. The Role of Ethical Leadership in Maintaining Market Integrity

At the core of any organization's effort to prevent insider trading is the **commitment to ethical leadership**. **CEOs, board members, and executives** must lead by example, creating a corporate culture that emphasizes **honesty** and **compliance**.

- **Ethical Decision-Making**: Organizations must ensure that **ethical decision-making** is a core component of their governance structure. Regular training, leadership accountability, and transparent communications are essential in cultivating an environment where compliance is not just a legal obligation but a **moral imperative**.

2. The Importance of Compliance in Maintaining Trust

Maintaining market integrity requires **consistent compliance** at both the individual and institutional levels. By embracing **proactive measures** such as **trading pre-clearance systems**, **whistleblower programs**, and **real-time surveillance technologies**, companies can safeguard against insider trading violations.

- **Restoring Investor Confidence**: When markets operate transparently, with clear regulations and rigorous enforcement, **investor confidence** is restored. This leads to healthier capital markets, where investments are driven by public information rather than secretive dealings.

3. The Path Forward for Global Markets

As markets continue to evolve, so too must the regulations and technologies used to protect them. The integration of **AI**, **blockchain**, and **global collaboration** will define the future of insider trading regulation, ensuring that **bad actors** are held accountable and that financial markets remain **fair and transparent** for all.

Conclusion: Ethical Compliance as the Foundation for Sustainable Markets

The journey to creating a compliant, ethical market is continuous. While regulations and technologies play critical roles in preventing and detecting insider trading, it is ultimately the **ethical behaviour** of professionals, investors, and corporations that will shape the future of financial markets. By fostering a culture of **transparency**, **integrity**, and **accountability**, we can collectively ensure that **financial markets** remain a place where **trust** and **fairness** are the foundation for economic growth.

Chapter 27

Appendix: Supporting Materials for Understanding Insider Trading

In this section, we provide additional resources to help deepen your understanding of insider trading regulations, policies, and key concepts. This includes a **Glossary of Terms**, a summary of **Insider Trading Regulations** from major jurisdictions like **India (SEBI), U.S. (SEC),** and **U.K. (FCA)**, a **Sample Insider Trading Policy for Corporates**, and **Key Resources for Further Reading**.

Glossary of Terms

- **Material Non-Public Information (MNPI):** Information that is not publicly available and could significantly affect a company's stock price or trading volume if disclosed.

- **Blackout Period:** A designated period, often before earnings announcements or major corporate events, during which corporate insiders are prohibited from trading company stock.

- **Pre-Clearance**: The process by which corporate insiders must obtain approval from their company's compliance or legal department before making trades in company stock.

- **Insider**: Any person who has access to confidential, non-public information about a company, including directors, officers, employees, or significant shareholders.

- **Rule 10b5-1 Plan**: A U.S. SEC rule that allows corporate insiders to establish pre-scheduled trading plans to avoid accusations of insider trading.

- **Trading Window**: A specified time period during which insiders are allowed to trade company shares, typically when there is no pending MNPI.

- **Whistleblower**: An individual who reports unethical or illegal activities, such as insider trading, often to regulatory authorities.

- **Forensic Accounting**: The use of accounting, auditing, and investigative skills to detect fraud or insider trading activities.

- **Integrated Market Surveillance System (IMSS)**: An automated system used by regulators like SEBI to monitor market trading activities for suspicious patterns that may indicate insider trading.

- **Market Maker**: A firm or individual that provides liquidity to markets by buying and selling securities and often holds inventories of stocks.

Insider Trading Regulations in Key Jurisdictions

1. India (SEBI: Securities and Exchange Board of India)

India's primary regulation on insider trading is governed by the **SEBI (Prohibition of Insider Trading) Regulations, 2015**. The regulations define **insider trading** as dealing in securities by any person who has access to **unpublished price-sensitive information (UPSI)**.

Key Provisions:

- **Insider Definition**: Anyone who has access to UPSI by virtue of their relationship with the company (e.g., directors, employees, auditors).

- **Prohibition on Trading**: Insiders are prohibited from trading in securities while in possession of UPSI.

- **Disclosure**: All insiders must disclose their trades to the company and the stock exchanges. Immediate disclosure of trades above a certain threshold is mandatory.

- **Trading Plans**: Similar to the U.S. Rule 10b5-1, SEBI allows insiders to create **trading plans** to trade securities without being suspected of insider trading, provided the plan is disclosed upfront and is adhered to strictly.

2. United States (SEC: Securities and Exchange Commission)

In the U.S., insider trading is regulated under the **Securities Exchange Act of 1934**, specifically under **Section 10(b)** and **Rule 10b-5**. This makes it unlawful for any person to engage in fraudulent or manipulative practices, including insider trading.

Key Provisions:

- **Material Information**: The SEC defines **material information** as anything that a reasonable investor would consider important in making an investment decision.

- **Prohibited Conduct**: Any insider who trades based on MNPI is subject to civil and criminal penalties, including fines and imprisonment.

- **Penalties**: Violators can face fines of up to **three times the profit gained** or **loss avoided** through insider trading, along with possible prison sentences of up to **20 years**.

- **Whistleblower Program**: The SEC incentivizes whistleblowers by offering **10%-30%** of monetary sanctions collected from enforcement actions based on their tips.

3. United Kingdom (FCA: Financial Conduct Authority)

In the U.K., insider trading is governed under the **Market Abuse Regulation (MAR)** and the **Criminal Justice Act of 1993**.

Key Provisions:

- **Market Abuse**: Under MAR, insider dealing is considered a form of market abuse. Insiders are prohibited from trading while in possession of confidential information.

- **Criminal Penalties**: The **Criminal Justice Act** provides for criminal prosecution of insider trading, with penalties including **up to 7 years in prison** and unlimited fines.

- **Disclosure Requirements**: Directors and certain employees must disclose their transactions in company shares.

- **Market Surveillance**: The FCA employs sophisticated surveillance mechanisms, including AI and big data analytics, to detect and investigate insider trading activities.

SAMPLE POLICY

Insider Trading Policy for Corporates

Insider Trading Policy for [Company Name]

Effective Date: [Insert Date]
Version: [Insert Version Number]
Approved by: Board of Directors, [Company Name]

1. Purpose and Scope

The purpose of this **Insider Trading Policy** (the "Policy") is to provide clear guidelines for all employees, directors, officers, and other relevant parties regarding trading in the securities of [Company Name] while in possession of **Material Non-Public Information (MNPI)**. The Policy is designed to ensure compliance with applicable insider trading laws, including the **Securities and Exchange Board of India (SEBI) Prohibition of Insider Trading Regulations, 2015**, and relevant international laws such as the **Securities and Exchange Commission (SEC) Rule 10b-5**.

This Policy applies to all employees, directors, officers, consultants, contractors, secondary market intermediaries, and any other person or entity with access to MNPI related to [Company Name] or its securities.

2. Key Definitions

- **Material Non-Public Information (MNPI):** Any information that is not public and is likely to affect the company's stock price or an investor's decision to buy or sell securities. Examples include unpublished financial results, mergers and acquisitions, product developments, and significant leadership changes.

- **Insider:** Anyone in possession of MNPI, including employees, directors, officers, consultants, and external advisers. Insiders are prohibited from using this information for personal financial gain.

- **Trading Window:** Specific periods during which insiders are permitted to buy, sell, or deal in company securities, provided they are not in possession of MNPI. Outside these periods, no trading is allowed.

- **Blackout Period:** A designated time frame during which trading in the company's securities is prohibited due to the pending release of material, non-public information.

3. Trading Guidelines

3.1. Prohibited Activities

- **No Trading on MNPI:** Insiders are strictly prohibited from trading in [Company Name]'s securities while in possession of MNPI. This includes any form of buying, selling, or dealing in the company's securities.

- **No Tipping:** Insiders are prohibited from disclosing MNPI to others, including family members, friends, or business associates, who may then use this information to trade. This act, known as "tipping," is also illegal under insider trading laws.

- **No Hedging or Derivative Transactions:** Insiders are prohibited from engaging in hedging or speculative transactions involving the company's securities, such as trading in options, derivatives, or other speculative instruments.

3.2. Pre-Clearance of Trades

- **Pre-Clearance Requirement:** Certain designated individuals (directors, senior executives, and key personnel with access to MNPI) must obtain pre-clearance from the **Compliance Officer** before executing any trade in the company's securities, regardless of whether the trading window is open.

- **Reporting of Trades:** All trades must be reported to the Compliance Officer within **48 hours** of execution.

4. Trading Windows and Blackout Periods

4.1. Trading Windows

- [Company Name] will establish **trading windows** during which insiders are allowed to trade, subject to pre-clearance, provided they are not in possession of MNPI. Trading windows will typically open for **10 days** following the public release of quarterly or annual earnings results.

4.2. Blackout Periods

- **Blackout periods** will be imposed in anticipation of significant corporate announcements, such as earnings releases, mergers, acquisitions, major business changes, or any other event likely to affect the stock price. During blackout periods, all trading in the company's securities is strictly prohibited.

- The Compliance Officer will notify insiders of the commencement and duration of blackout periods.

5. Compliance Monitoring and Responsibilities

5.1. Compliance Officer

- A **Compliance Officer** will be appointed to oversee the implementation of this Policy, monitor compliance, and address any issues related to insider trading. The Compliance Officer will maintain records of all pre-clearance requests, trade reports, and compliance violations.

5.2. Reporting Violations

- Any suspected violations of this Policy must be reported immediately to the Compliance Officer. Reports will be treated confidentially, and the company guarantees that there will be no retaliation against employees who report concerns in good faith.

6. Legal Consequences and Penalties

6.1. Company Penalties

- Violations of this Policy or applicable insider trading laws may result in severe disciplinary action, including termination of employment. In addition, the company reserves the right to take legal action against any individual found to have violated this Policy.

6.2. Regulatory and Criminal Penalties

- Under **SEBI** regulations, individuals found guilty of insider trading may face civil penalties up to ₹25 crore or three times the profit made or loss avoided, whichever is higher. In the U.S., the **SEC** imposes fines of up to $5 million and imprisonment of up to 20 years for insider trading offenses.

- Criminal prosecution may also result in imprisonment, fines, and the forfeiture of any ill-gotten gains. In addition to legal sanctions, violators face reputational damage, loss of professional licenses, and other long-term career consequences.

7. Secondary Market Intermediaries and Consultants

7.1. Responsibilities of Market Intermediaries

- **Brokers, custodians, investment advisors, and other intermediaries** who facilitate trading in the company's securities are expected to adhere to the company's Policy and any applicable insider trading regulations.

- **Monitoring of Client Trades:** Market intermediaries must have systems in place to monitor trading patterns for suspicious activity and report any suspected insider trading to regulatory authorities, such as SEBI, SEC, or FCA.

7.2. Consultants and External Advisors

- Consultants, contractors, or third-party advisors with access to MNPI are also subject to this Policy and may not trade in the company's securities or disclose MNPI.

8. Whistleblower Provisions

- **Whistleblower Protections:** Employees and other insiders who report violations of this Policy are protected under the company's whistleblower protection policy. Retaliation against whistleblowers is strictly prohibited.

- **Anonymous Reporting:** Individuals may report concerns regarding insider trading violations anonymously via the company's whistleblower hotline or confidential reporting system.

9. Employee Education and Training

- **Mandatory Training:** All employees and relevant stakeholders will undergo mandatory training on insider trading laws and the company's Policy. Annual refresher courses will be provided to ensure continued compliance.

- **Employee Acknowledgement:** All insiders must sign an acknowledgment form confirming they have read and understood this Policy.

10. Policy Amendments

This Policy may be amended or updated by [Company Name] at any time to comply with changes in law, regulations, or best practices. Any changes will be communicated promptly to all relevant parties.

Compliance Officer Contact Information:
Name: [Insert Name]
Email: [Insert Email]
Phone: [Insert Phone Number]

Acknowledgment:
I have received, read, and understood the Insider Trading Policy of [Company Name].
Name: [Insert Name]
Signature: _____
Date: _____

SAMPLE TRAINING MANNUAL

Employee Training Manual on Insider Trading for [Company Name]

Introduction

Welcome to [Company Name]'s **Insider Trading Compliance Training**. This manual provides a comprehensive guide on insider trading laws, policies, and best practices to ensure that all employees, directors, and other stakeholders are well-equipped to understand and comply with both **legal requirements** and the **corporate policies** designed to prevent insider trading.

This training aims to ensure that everyone within the company understands their responsibility in protecting the integrity of the financial markets and avoiding the severe consequences of insider trading violations.

Table of Contents

1. What is Insider Trading?
2. Importance of Compliance and Ethical Conduct

3. **Understanding Material Non-Public Information (MNPI)**
4. **Company's Insider Trading Policy Overview**
   - Trading Windows and Blackout Periods
   - Pre-Clearance Procedures
   - Prohibited Activities
5. **Consequences of Insider Trading Violations**
   - Legal Penalties
   - Company Penalties
6. **Reporting Suspected Insider Trading**
   - Whistleblower Protections
7. **Practical Scenarios and Examples**
8. **Employee Acknowledgment and Certification**

1. What is Insider Trading?

Insider trading refers to the buying or selling of securities while in possession of **Material Non-Public Information (MNPI)** about a company. MNPI is any information that could significantly affect the company's stock price if it were made public. Trading on this information is both unethical and illegal, as it provides an unfair advantage to insiders over general market participants.

Examples of **insider trading** include:

- Buying or selling stocks based on confidential information about an upcoming merger, earnings report, or product launch.

- Disclosing MNPI to family, friends, or business partners so they can trade on the information ("tipping").

2. Importance of Compliance and Ethical Conduct

Compliance with insider trading laws and regulations is **crucial** for maintaining market integrity, protecting [Company Name]'s reputation, and avoiding legal consequences. This training emphasizes the ethical standards expected from every employee, ensuring that [Company Name] fosters a culture of **transparency, fairness, and accountability**.

3. Understanding Material Non-Public Information (MNPI)

Material Non-Public Information (MNPI) refers to any information that has not been publicly disclosed and could influence an investor's decision to buy or sell securities. Examples of MNPI include:

- Unreleased financial results or earnings reports.
- Pending mergers, acquisitions, or sales of major assets.
- Product developments, such as new technology or patent filings.
- Changes in senior management or the board of directors.
- Major legal disputes or regulatory actions.

To avoid insider trading violations, employees must understand whether the information they possess qualifies as MNPI and take appropriate action by refraining from trading or sharing it.

4. Company's Insider Trading Policy Overview

4.1. Trading Windows and Blackout Periods

- **Trading Windows**: Employees, directors, and designated insiders are only permitted to trade in

[Company Name] securities during approved **trading windows**—typically a set period following the public release of quarterly or annual earnings reports. Trading outside these windows is prohibited.

- **Blackout Periods**: During certain sensitive times, such as before earnings releases or major announcements, the company will enforce **blackout periods**, during which all trading by insiders is strictly prohibited.

4.2. Pre-Clearance Procedures

- **Pre-Clearance**: Key insiders (such as directors, executives, and designated employees) must seek **pre-clearance** from the Compliance Officer before initiating any trade in company securities, even during open trading windows.

4.3. Prohibited Activities

The following activities are strictly prohibited under the company's Insider Trading Policy:

- **Trading on MNPI**: Buying, selling, or otherwise trading company securities while in possession of MNPI.

- **Tipping**: Sharing MNPI with third parties, including family members, friends, or business associates, who might use that information to trade.

- **Short-Selling and Speculative Trading**: Engaging in short-selling, derivative transactions, or other speculative trades in [Company Name]'s securities.

5. Consequences of Insider Trading Violations

5.1. Legal Penalties

Violations of insider trading laws can lead to severe civil and criminal penalties, including:

- **Fines**: Under **SEBI** regulations, individuals may face fines up to ₹25 crore or three times the profit made, whichever is higher. In the U.S., the **SEC** can impose fines of up to $5 million.
- **Imprisonment**: Insider trading violations may result in imprisonment, with sentences of up to 20 years in the U.S.

5.2. Company Penalties

Violators of the company's Insider Trading Policy may also face serious consequences, including:

- **Termination of Employment**: Employees found guilty of insider trading will face immediate dismissal.
- **Disciplinary Action**: Non-compliance with this policy may result in disciplinary action, including legal referrals and market bans.
- **Reputational Damage**: Violating insider trading laws can severely damage your professional and personal reputation.

6. Reporting Suspected Insider Trading

Employees are encouraged to report any suspicious activity or potential violations of the company's Insider Trading Policy. Reports can be made confidentially to the **Compliance Officer**.

6.1. Whistleblower Protections Whistleblower Protections:

Employees who report suspected violations in good faith are protected under [Company Name]'s whistleblower policy. Retaliation against whistleblowers is strictly prohibited.

6.2. How to Report a Violation

Employees can report violations to the Compliance Officer via:

Email: [Insert Email Address]

Anonymous Hotline: [Insert Hotline Number]

In-Person: At the Compliance Office located at [Insert Office Location]

7. Practical Scenarios and Examples

Scenario 1: Trading on Unreleased Financial Results You overhear a conversation about [Company Name] reporting better-than-expected quarterly earnings next week. You're tempted to buy company stock before the announcement. **Is this allowed?**

Answer: No, this is considered insider trading because the financial results have not yet been made public.

Scenario 2: Tipping a Friend Your friend asks about a potential merger involving [Company Name], and you have access to MNPI on the deal. Can you share this information with your friend so they can make a profitable trade?

Answer: No, this would be considered "tipping," which is a violation of both company policy and insider trading laws.

Scenario 3: Trading During a Blackout Period You want to sell some of your company stock during a blackout period due to personal financial reasons. Can you request an exemption?

Answer: No, trading during blackout periods is prohibited, even for personal financial needs. You must wait until the blackout period is lifted.

8. Employee Acknowledgment and Certification

All employees are required to acknowledge and certify their understanding of the Insider Trading Policy by signing the form below.

Insider Trading Policy Acknowledgment Form

I, [Insert Name], have read and understood the **Insider Trading Policy** and **Training Manual** provided by [Company Name]. I understand the rules regarding the handling of **Material Non-Public Information (MNPI)**, and I agree to comply with the company's Insider Trading Policy. I understand that any violation of this Policy may result in severe disciplinary action, including termination of employment and legal penalties.

Name: _____
Position: _____
Signature: _____
Date: _____

Key Resources for Further Reading

1. Books:
   - "The Laws of Insider Trading: An Analytical Guide" by Stephen M. Bainbridge A comprehensive book that provides insights into the complexities of insider trading laws and their practical application in various jurisdictions.

   - "White-Collar Crime and Insider Trading: An Analysis of Insider Trading Regulation" by Samuel W. Buell
   A critical exploration of white-collar crime and insider trading, offering an analysis of regulatory responses to insider trading globally.

2. References:
   1. SEBI (Prohibition of Insider Trading) Regulations, 2015
   2. NSE Circulars on Insider Trading
   3. BSE Listing Obligations and Disclosure Requirements Regulations, 2015

3. Research Papers:
   - "The Effectiveness of Insider Trading Regulations in Emerging Markets" by Tarun Khanna, Keshub

Mahindra Chair, A deep dive into how insider trading regulations have evolved in emerging markets like India and China and the effectiveness of these regulations.

- **"Insider Trading: Economics, Politics, and Regulation"** by Henry G. Manne An influential paper examining the economic implications of insider trading, its regulation, and the political landscape shaping its enforcement.

4. Websites and Online Resources:

- **SEC Insider Trading Page**
  Official page for insider trading resources and updates from the U.S. Securities and Exchange Commission: www.sec.gov

- **SEBI - Insider Trading Regulations**
  Access the latest insider trading regulations in India from SEBI: www.sebi.gov.in

- **FCA Market Abuse Regulation**
  Explore the FCA's official resources on Market Abuse Regulation (MAR): www.fca.org.uk

- SEBI (Prohibition of Insider Trading) Regulations, 2015. Retrieved from https://www.sebi.gov.in/legal/regulations/dec-2014/sebi-prohibition-of-insider-trading-regulations-2015-last-amended-on-june-17-2020-_33730.html

- Code of Conduct for Prevention of Insider Trading. Retrieved from https://www.tcs.com/content/dam/tcs/investor-relations/pdf/code-of-conduct-insider-trading.pdf

- Insider Trading Policy. Retrieved from https://www.infosys.com/investors/corporate-governance/Documents/Insider-Trading-Policy.pdf
- Securities and Exchange Board of India (SEBI), "Prohibition of Insider Trading Regulations, 2015," https://www.sebi.gov.in/legal/regulations/oct-2015/prohibition-of-insider-trading-regulations-2015-last-amended-on-march-17-2020-_34644.html
- National Stock Exchange of India (NSE), "Prevention of Insider Trading Policy," https://www.nseindia.com/content/circulars/CMPT40906.zip
- BSE Limited, "Code of Conduct for Prevention of Insider Trading," https://www.bseindia.com/downloads1/Code_of_Conduct_for_Prevention_of_Insider_Trading.pdf

www.ingramcontent.com/pod-product-compliance
Ingram Content Group UK Ltd.
Pitfield, Milton Keynes, MK11 3LW, UK
UKHW020243240426
12048UKWH00026B/1584